200 Fast

vegetarian recipes

200 *Fast*
vegetarian recipes
hamlyn **all color**

An Hachette UK Company
www.hachette.co.uk

First published in Great Britain in 2015 by Hamlyn
a division of Octopus Publishing Group Ltd,
Carmelite House, 50 Victoria Embankment,
London EC4Y 0DZ

www.octopusbooks.co.uk
www.octopusbooksusa.com

Copyright © Octopus Publishing Group Ltd 2015

Some of the recipes in this book have previously appeared
in other titles published by Hamlyn.

Distributed in the US by Hachette Book Group
1290 Avenue of the Americas, 4th and 5th Floors,
New York, NY 10020

Distributed in Canada by Canadian Manda Group,
664 Annette St., Toronto, Ontario, Canada M6S 2C8

ISBN 13: 978-0-600-63090-6

Printed and bound in China.

1 2 3 4 5 6 7 8 9 10

Standard level kitchen spoon and cup measurements
are used in all recipes.

Ovens should be preheated to the specified temperature;
if using a convection oven, follow the manufacturer's
instructions for adjusting the time and temperature.

Fresh herbs should be used unless otherwise stated.

Eggs should be large unless otherwise stated. The U.S.
Food and Drug Administration advises that eggs should not
be consumed raw. This book contains dishes made with
raw or lightly cooked eggs. It is prudent for more vulnerable
people, such as pregnant and nursing mothers, people with
weakened immune systems, the elderly, babies, and young
children, to avoid uncooked or lightly cooked dishes made
with eggs. Once prepared, these dishes should be kept
refrigerated and used promptly.

This book includes dishes made with nuts and nut
derivatives. It is advisable for customers with known allergic
reactions to nuts and nut derivatives and those who may be
potentially vulnerable to these allergies, such as pregnant
and nursing mothers, people with weakened immune
systems, the elderly, babies, and children, to avoid dishes
made with nuts and nut oils. It is also prudent to check the
labels of prepared ingredients for the possible inclusion of
nut derivatives.

contents

introduction

This book offers a new and flexible approach to planning meals for busy cooks and lets you choose the recipe option that best fits the time you have available. Inside you will find 200 dishes that will inspire you and motivate you to get cooking every day of the year.

All the recipes take a maximum of 30 minutes to cook. Some take as little as 20 minutes and, amazingly, many take only 10 minutes.

On every page, you'll find a main recipe plus a short-cut version or a fancier variation if you have a little extra time on hand. Whatever you choose, you'll find a huge range of superquick recipes to get you through the week.

vegetarian recipes

A diet rich in fresh vegetables, beans, and whole grains is well documented to be a healthy one. Armed with the knowledge that a diet high in meat protein can be detrimental to health, and with such an abundance of wonderful, seasonal vegetables widely available, it's not difficult to understand why many people choose to follow a vegetarian or "flexitarian" diet.

The key to a well-balanced vegetarian diet is simple: eat plenty of whole grains (brown rice, barley, corn, oats, millet, and buckwheat are all good options), foods that are made from whole grains (such as whole-grain breads, pastas, and cereals), protein-rich beans and other legumes, lentils, nuts, and eggs, and an abundance of fresh fruit and vegetables. Dairy products (such as butter, cheese, cream, milk, and yogurt) or nondairy alternatives should form a smaller part of the diet and caffeinated beverages, alcohol, and sugary treats should be enjoyed in moderation.

Complex carbohydrates are essential for a good diet and vital for energy. The presence of dietary fiber allows the energy from the natural sugars they contain to be released slowly, as opposed to refined sugars, which are released into the body quickly and can leave energy levels depleted. Foods rich in complex carbohydrates include those made using the whole of the grain, such as whole-grain bread and whole wheat pasta, as well as brown rice, barley, corn, buckwheat, dried beans, and bananas.

A healthy vegetarian diet will be high in fiber, which is vital for moving the food in the bowel, helping to prevent intestinal problems and reducing the risk of bowel cancer. Foods rich in fiber can help to lower blood cholesterol; therefore, it is advisable to include high-fiber foods, such as beans and peas, brassica family vegetables (including cabbage, broccoli, and Brussels sprouts), oats, and whole wheat, in most of your meals.

Protein is essential for tissue repair and cell growth and reproduction, especially for growing children and pregnant women. However, we do not need large amounts of protein in our diet, and it is perfectly possible to consume the recommended amounts of protein from just nonanimal foods. Good sources of vegetarian protein include nuts and seeds, legumes (such as beans, chickpeas, and peas), lentils, and soy products.

techniques and tips

Using condiments, seasonings, herbs and spices can liven up your dining experience enormously, giving you an opportunity to cook and eat a glorious palette of flavors, colors, and textures. Stock up your pantry and refrigerator before you begin to travel through the varied and wonderful world of vegetarian cooking. Most supermarkets will sell everything you'll need, but also try ethnic food stores and farmers' markets to source more unusual ingredients and produce.

A well-equipped kitchen will really help you to save time when preparing your vegetarian meals. A couple of good saucepans of different sizes, a skillet, and a wok are all essentials, and you will find plenty of uses for a good-quality mortar and pestle. A salad spinner speeds up salad washing, and kitchen measuring cups and spoons for accurate measuring will help you achieve successful results every time. A food processor is a must for quick and easy blending and processing.

red lentils, and yellow split peas, are essential for creating delicious vegetarian dishes, and canned legumes and beans are handy for quick last-minute meals. A good supply of kidney beans, chickpeas, black-eyed peas, and cannellini beans will also be really useful.

Healthy, wholesome, and delicious, nuts and seeds will perk up many dishes from salads to stir-fries. Sunflower seeds, sesame seeds, cashew nuts, almonds, pistachio, and walnuts make nutritious additions to vegetarian meals.

Packed with flavor and color, canned tomatoes and tomato puree or sauce have a multitude of uses and are a terrific standby for making quick sauces, casseroles, and stews.

Good-quality olive oil, sunflower oil, vegetable oil, and toasted sesame seed oil are great for stir-frying and general-purpose cooking. Red wine, white wine, balsamic, apple cider, and rice wine vinegars are a must for creating quick salad dressings and sauces.

pantry staples

It's a good idea to have a variety of dried pasta shapes on hand. Linguini, spaghetti, pappardelle, fusilli, penne, and orzo should cover most recipes.

Rice (basmati or other long-grain, brown, jasmine, risotto, and paella), bulgur, couscous, cornmeal, and quinoa are great staples that can be used in a variety of ways to produce wonderful, quick meals. All-purpose flour is a must for making sauce bases and crumb toppings. Chickpea (besan) flour is great for a spiced batter base for crispy vegetable fritters.

Quick-cooking legumes that don't require long soaking, such as dried green lentils, split

flavorings
You cannot have enough of a variety of dried herbs and spices in your pantry to experiment with flavors. The list is endless, but always remember to buy them in small quantities and use within three months for maximum flavor. A good stock of dried herbs (basil, thyme, oregano, tarragon, rosemary, and parsley are a good starting point), whole spices (cumin seeds, coriander seeds, black mustard seeds, cloves, cardamom pods, and cinnamon

sticks) and ground spices (cumin, cinnamon, coriander, chili powder, paprika, and turmeric) will really add depth to your dishes. Sea salt and fresh black peppercorns are also a must.

Stock up on a selection of sauces and condiments to add instant flavor to your dishes. Soy sauce, sweet chili sauce, Tabasco sauce, and Worcestershire sauce are staples you will use time and time again. Honey and maple syrup are good sweeteners to keep on hand for both sweet and savory recipes.

fresh food

Keeping your refrigerator well stocked will enable you to create healthy and tasty vegetarian meals in minutes. The key is to buy fresh produce regularly, and to only buy what you know you will use to minimize wastage. Fresh pasta, tofu, cheese, butter, milk, cream, and eggs are always great to have in the refrigerator. You'll also find lemons, limes, red chiles, fresh ginger, scallions, and fresh herbs, such as cilantro, flat leaf parsley, and basil, are excellent additions to speedy meals.

Buy fruit and vegetables that are in season and, if possible, locally grown. The goodness and flavor will be far superior to those that have been grown out of season or have traveled many miles to reach the supermarket shelves. Garlic, onions, potatoes, shallots, carrots, and other root vegetables and most varieties of fruit will keep well for a few days in the pantry.

snacks &
light bites

quick quesadillas

Serves **4**

Total cooking time **10 minutes**

1 cup **refried beans**

8 **soft flour tortillas**

¼ cup drained **jalapeño pepper slices**

1 **large tomato**, seeded and diced

1 ½ cups shredded **cheddar cheese**

2 **scallions**, sliced

1 tablespoon finely chopped **fresh cilantro** (optional)

½ cup **sour cream,** to serve (optional)

Spread the refried beans over 4 of the tortillas. Top with the jalapeño slices, diced tomato, shredded cheese, scallions, and chopped cilantro, if using. Cover each one with another tortilla to make 4 quesadillas.

Toast the quesadillas, one at a time, in a large ridged grill pan set over a medium-high heat for 30–60 seconds on each side, until lightly browned and the cheese inside has melted.

Cut the quesadillas into quarters and serve immediately with sour cream, if using.

For spicy bean burritos, spread the refried beans over all 8 tortillas, then top with the jalapeño slices, 2 large, diced tomatoes, 1 cored, seeded, and chopped red bell pepper, and the sliced scallion. Tuck in the ends and roll each tortilla tightly, then place in a snug-fitting ovenproof dish. Pour 1 cup store-bought spicy salsa over the tortillas, then dot with small spoonfuls of sour cream and sprinkle with the cheese. Cook in a preheated oven, at 425°F, for 20–25 minutes, until hot and bubbling. Serve hot with shredded iceberg lettuce and the chopped cilantro, if using. **Total cooking time 30 minutes.**

stuffed zucchini

Serves **4**
Total cooking time **30 minutes**

4 **zucchini**
3 **plum tomatoes**, chopped
1¾ cups shredded
   mozzarella cheese
2 tablespoons shredded **basil**
¼ cup grated **Parmesan
   cheese**
salt and **black pepper**

Slice the zucchini in half horizontally and then scoop out the middle of each one, reserving the flesh.

Place the zucchini halves in a roasting pan, cut side up, and bake in a preheated oven, at 400°F, for 10 minutes.

Meanwhile, chop the reserved zucchini flesh and mix it in a bowl with the chopped tomatoes, shredded mozzarella, and basil. Season.

Remove the zucchini halves from the oven and spoon the filling into each one.

Sprinkle with the grated Parmesan and return to the oven to bake for 15 minutes, until golden.

For grilled zucchini with mozzarella, use a vegetable peeler to thinly slice 4 zucchini lengthwise. Toss the zucchini in 2 tablespoons olive oil and then cook them on a preheated hot ridged grill pan for 2–3 minutes on both sides, until grill marks start to show. Served topped with 7 oz mozzarella cheese, torn into pieces, and 6–8 torn basil. Drizzle with a little olive oil and a squeeze of lemon juice, and season with black pepper. **Total cooking time 20 minutes.**

asparagus frittata

Serves **4**
Total cooking time **30 minutes**

12 oz **asparagus**
2 tablespoons **olive oil**
6 **extra-large eggs**
½ cup grated **Parmesan cheese**
1 tablespoon chopped **oregano**
salt and **black pepper**

Break the woody ends off the asparagus and discard. Toss the spears in 1 tablespoon of the olive oil.

Heat a ridged grill pan until hot and cook the asparagus for 4–5 minutes, until starting to look a little charred. Cut the asparagus spears into thirds.

Beat the eggs in a large mixing bowl with the grated Parmesan, oregano, and some salt and black pepper. Add the asparagus.

Heat the remaining oil in a flameproof, nonstick skillet. Pour the mixture into the pan and cook for 8–10 minutes over low heat, tipping the pan from time to time to let the runny egg reach the edges to cook evenly.

Cook under a preheated hot broiler for an additional 4–5 minutes, until the top is golden.

Turn the frittata out onto a board, cut into wedges, and serve immediately.

For grilled asparagus, toss 1 lb trimmed asparagus in 2 tablespoons olive oil. Heat a ridged grill pan until hot and cook the asparagus for 4–5 minutes, turning once. Serve drizzled with olive oil and sprinkled with Parmesan cheese shavings. **Total cooking time 10 minutes.**

falafel with spicy sauce

Serves **4**

Total cooking time **15 minutes**

1 (15 oz) **can chickpeas (garbanzo beans)**, rinsed and drained

1 **onion**, finely diced

2 **garlic** cloves, chopped

3 tablespoons chopped **parsley**

1 teaspoon **ground coriander**

1 teaspoon **ground cumin**

2 tablespoons **all-purpose flour**

2–3 tablespoons **vegetable oil**

salt and **black pepper**

½ i**ceburg lettuce**, shredded, to serve

Spicy sauce

⅓ cup **tomato paste**

½–1 teaspoon **harissa paste**, to taste

2 **garlic cloves**, crushed

1 teaspoon **lemon juice**

¼ cup **water**

1 tablespoon chopped **parsley**

To make the sauce, place all the ingredients into a small saucepan and simmer for 10 minutes.

Meanwhile, put all the falafel ingredients except the oil into a large bowl and mash together with a fork. Season. Alternatively, place the ingredients in a food processor and process until smooth. Using wet hands, shape the mixture into small balls and flatten slightly.

Heat the vegetable oil in a skillet and cook the falafel for 5–7 minutes, turning once, until golden all over.

Serve on the lettuce with the spicy sauce.

For falafel & tabbouleh salad, make the falafel as above. Meanwhile, put 1½ cups couscous into a heatproof bowl and just cover with boiling water. Let stand for 10 minutes. Fluff up the couscous with a fork, then stir in 2 tablespoons each of chopped mint, parsley, and chives, 3 diced tomatoes, and ½ diced cucumber. Serve with the falafel and dollops of store-bought hummus. **Total cooking time 20 minutes.**

eggplant melts

Serves **4**

Total cooking time **30 minutes**

2 **eggplants**, halved
   lengthwise
¼ cup **olive oil**
4 **tomatoes**, sliced
8 oz **mozzarella cheese**,
   sliced
a small handful of **basil**
2 tablespoons **toasted
   pine nuts**
black pepper
crisp **green salad**, to serve

Place the eggplant halves on a baking sheet, drizzle with the olive oil, and bake in a preheated oven, at 400°F, for 20 minutes, until softened.

Remove the eggplant from the oven, arrange the slices of tomato and mozzarella on top, and bake for an additional 5 minutes, until the cheese has melted.

Sprinkle with basil and pine nuts, season with black pepper, and serve with a crisp green salad.

For eggplant & goat cheese pasta, cook 1 lb pasta shapes of your choice in a saucepan of boiling water, according to the package directions, until "al dente." Meanwhile, heat 1 tablespoon olive oil in a skillet and sauté 1 chopped onion and 2 sliced garlic cloves for 3–4 minutes. Add 1 chopped eggplant and cook for an additional 4–5 minutes. Pour in 1 (14½ oz) can diced tomatoes and simmer for 3–4 minutes. Drain the pasta and stir into the sauce with 4 oz crumbled goat cheese and a small handful of torn basil and mix well. **Total cooking time 20 minutes.**

corn fritters with salsa

Serves **4**
Total cooking time **20 minutes**

1 (8¾ oz) **can corn kernels**
½ cup **all-purpose flour**
1 teaspoon **baking powder**
1 **egg**, beaten
½ **red bell pepper**, cored,
  seeded, and finely chopped
1 small **red chile,** seeded and
  finely chopped
⅓ cup chopped **fresh cilantro**
2 tablespoons **vegetable oil**
black pepper

Salsa
1 tablespoon **olive oil**
2 **tomatoes**, finely chopped
½ small **red chile,** finely
  chopped
1 tablespoon packed
  light brown sugar
2 tablespoons chopped
  fresh cilantro

Drain the corn, put half the kernels into a food processor, and process until almost smooth. Transfer to a bowl and stir in the remaining whole corn kernels. Sift in the flour and baking powder and mix together. Mix in the egg, red bell pepper, chile, and cilantro and season with plenty of black pepper.

Heat the oil in a large, heavy nonstick skillet over medium-high heat and drop in 4 spoonfuls of the batter. Cook for about 1 minute on each side, until browned. Remove with a spatula, drain on paper towels, and keep warm. Cook the remaining batter in the same way (to make 8 fritters in total).

Meanwhile, mix together all the ingredients for the salsa, season with black pepper, and transfer to a serving bowl.

Serve the fritters warm with the salsa on the side.

For corn pancakes, make up 1 cup complete pancake mix according to the package directions, then mix in ½ cup drained canned corn kernels and 3 tablespoons chopped fresh cilantro. Season well. Heat a little vegetable oil in a skillet over medium-high heat, pour in one-quarter of the batter, and cook for 1 minute, then turn and cook for a few seconds on the other side. Cook the remaining batter in the same way. Fill the pancakes with store-bought salsa and a few arugula leaves, if desired. **Total cooking time 10 minutes.**

tostados with avocado & tomato

Serves **4**

Total cooking time **10 minutes**

4 **corn tortillas**

1 tablespoon **vegetable oil**

2 **avocados**, peeled and pitted

¼ cup **sour cream** or **crème fraîche**

2–3 tablespoons **lime juice**

4 **tomatoes**, chopped

1 tablespoon finely chopped **red onion**

1 tablespoon **extra virgin olive oil**

handful of **fresh cilantro**, chopped, plus extra to serve (optional)

salt and **black pepper**

Use a 2 inch cookie cutter to stamp out disks from the tortillas; alternatively, cut them into wedges. Brush them with vegetable oil, place on a baking sheet under a preheated hot broiler, and cook for 1 minute on each side until crisp. Let cool.

Meanwhile, put the avocado flesh and sour cream or crème fraîche into a food processor and process until smooth. Stir in 1 tablespoon of lime juice and season. Stir together the tomatoes, onion, and olive oil, add lime juice to taste, season, and stir through the cilantro.

Spoon a little of the avocado mixture onto each tortilla disk, sprinkle with the tomato salsa, and top with more cilantro, if desired.

For tomato & tortilla soup, heat 1 tablespoon olive oil in a saucepan, add 1 finely chopped onion, and cook for 5 minutes, until softened. Add 3 finely chopped garlic cloves and stir around the pan. Add 2 teaspoons chipotle paste, 1 (14½ oz) can diced tomatoes, 1 teaspoon packed brown sugar, and a pinch of dried oregano. Pour over 4 cups vegetable broth, bring to a boil, reduce the heat, and simmer for 10 minutes. Use an immersion blender to blend together until smooth, then season. Cut 2 corn tortillas into thin strips. Heat a large skillet, add 1 tablespoon vegetable oil, and cook the tortillas for 1–2 minutes, until golden and crisp. Spoon the soup into bowls. Top with the chopped flesh of 1 avocado, ⅓ cup crumbled feta cheese, the crisp tortillas, and a handful of chopped fresh cilantro. **Total cooking time 30 minutes.**

mozzarella & spinach crepes

Serves **4**

Total cooking time **20 minutes**

1 cup **all-purpose flour**
a pinch of **salt**
2 **eggs**
1 cup **milk** mixed with
⅓ cup **water**
4 tablespoons **butter**, melted
1 (6 oz) package **baby
spinach**
4 **tomatoes**, sliced
12 oz **mozzarella cheese**,
sliced
2 tablespoons grated
Parmesan cheese

Sift the flour and salt into a large bowl. Make a well in the center and break the eggs into it. Whisk the eggs into the flour and then gradually add a small amount of the milk and water, still whisking.

Whisk half the melted butter into the batter and use the remainder to grease a skillet. Rub the pan with paper towels to remove any excess.

Pour about 2 tablespoons of the batter into the pan and swirl around to completely coat the bottom. After 1 minute, check that the crepe (a thin French-style pancake) is cooked underneath and then flip it over to cook the other side for just a few more seconds.

Sprinkle half the crepe with some spinach, sliced tomatoes, and sliced mozzarella. Fold the other half of the crepe over the filled side and press lightly. Transfer the filled crepe to an ovenproof dish and keep warm.

Repeat with the remaining ingredients. Sprinkle the pancakes with the grated Parmesan and briefly cook under a preheated hot broiler until the pancakes are golden. Serve immediately.

For mozzarella & spinach salad, layer 3½ cups fresh spinach with 12 oz sliced mozzarella cheese, 2 thinly sliced beefsteak tomatoes, and 10–12 basil leaves on a large plate. Sprinkle with 2 teaspoons chopped oregano and 2 tablespoons toasted pine nuts and drizzle with 3 tablespoons extra virgin olive oil and 1 tablespoon balsamic vinegar. **Total cooking time 10 minutes.**

bocconcini with pesto mayo

Serves **4**
Total cooking time **20 minutes**

2 cups **fresh white
  bread crumbs**
zest of 1 **lemon**, finely grated
generous pinch of **dried red
  pepper flakes**
2 tablespoons **thyme**
⅓ cup **all-purpose flour**
2 **extra-large eggs**, beaten
10 oz **bocconcini (baby
  mozzarella balls)**, drained
vegetable oil, for deep-frying
salt and **black pepper**

Pesto mayonnaise
⅓ cup **fresh store-bought
  green pesto**
1 cup **mayonnaise**
2 **garlic cloves**, crushed

Make the pesto mayonnaise by mixing together all the
ingredients. Set aside.

Mix together the bread crumbs, lemon zest, a few dried
red pepper flakes, a sprinkling of the thyme, and some
seasoning in a medium bowl. Put the flour into a second
bowl and the eggs in a third.

Pat the mozzarella balls dry with paper towels. First
roll the balls in flour, then dip in the egg, then roll in
the bread crumb mixture. Repeat in the egg and bread
crumbs to create a double layer.

Fill a saucepan or deep fryer halfway with vegetable
oil. Just before serving, heat over high heat to 350°F
or until a cube of bread sizzles and turns golden in
10–15 seconds. Using a strainer or slotted spoon,
lower batches of the crumbed mozzarella into the
hot oil and fry for 3–4 minutes, until golden brown.
Remove and drain on paper towels.

Serve immediately with the fresh pesto aïoli.

For tomato, bocconcini & basil tricolore salad,
slice 4 tomatoes and put into a wide salad bowl with
a small handful basil and 10 oz bocconcini. Drizzle with
¼ cup extra virgin olive oil and squeeze with the juice
of 1 lemon. Season well and serve with ciabatta bread.
Total cooking time 10 minutes.

eggs florentine

Serves **4**
Total cooking time **10 minutes**

1 tablespoon **butter**, plus extra
   for buttering the muffins
½ bunch (about 6 oz) **spinach**
4 **English muffins**, halved
4 **eggs**
3 tablespoons chopped
   parsley
1 cup **hollandaise sauce**
salt and **black pepper**

Fill a small saucepan halfway with water and bring to
a boil. Meanwhile, melt the butter in a large saucepan,
add the spinach, and cook over medium heat, stirring,
for 1–2 minutes, until wilted. Season with salt and
black pepper.

Toast the English muffins, cut side up, under a reheated
medium broiler until lightly browned. Meanwhile, poach
the eggs, 2 at a time, in the boiling water and cook for
1–2 minutes, until the whites are firm and the yolks soft.

Butter the warm English muffins, then divide the spinach
among them and top with an egg. Mix the parsley into
the hollandaise and spoon the sauce over the eggs.
Top with black pepper and serve immediately.

For eggs Florentine with leek & cheese sauce, melt
2 tablespoons butter in a saucepan and cook 2 finely
sliced leeks over medium heat, stirring, for 3–4 minutes
until soft and beginning to brown. Stir in 3 tablespoons
all-purpose flour, then remove from the heat and add
1¾ cups milk, a little at a time, blending well between
each addition. Add 1 teaspoon prepared English mustard
and stir well, then return to the heat and bring to a boil,
stirring constantly, until thickened. Stir in 2 tablespoons
freshly grated Parmesan cheese. Cook and prepare
the spinach, eggs, and English muffins as above, then
assemble with the leek and cheese sauce instead of the
parsley hollandaise, serving with extra grated Parmesan,
if desired. **Total cooking time 20 minutes.**

scallion hash browns with salsa

Serves **4**
Total cooking time **30 minutes**

6 (1½ lb) **russet** or **Yukon Gold potatoes,** boiled
6 **scallions**, finely chopped
2 **garlic cloves**, minced
1 **extra-large egg**, lightly beaten
¼ cup **sunflower oil**
lime wedges, to serve (optional)

Salsa
2 **plum tomatoes**, seeded and coarsely chopped
1 **red chile,** seeded and finely chopped
1 small **red onion**, halved and thinly sliced
¼ cup finely chopped **fresh cilantro**
2 **avocados**, peeled, pitted, and coarsely sliced
juice of 2 **limes**
1 tablespoon **avocado oil**
salt and **black pepper**

Make the salsa by mixing all the ingredients together in a bowl. Season well and set aside until ready to serve.

Peel and coarsely grate the potatoes. Add the scallions, garlic, and egg and use your fingers to combine the mixture evenly.

Heat a large, nonstick skillet over high heat and add half of the oil.

Divide the potato mixture into 8 portions. Working in batches, spoon 4 of the portions into the oil and pat down to form patties 3–4 inches in diameter. Cook for 3–4 minutes on each side, then carefully transfer to a large, nonstick baking sheet. Repeat with the remaining oil and potato mixture to make 8 hash browns.

Serve the hash browns accompanied by the salsa and the lime wedges, if desired.

For scallion & potato soup, put 12 sliced scallions, 2 cups cooked, cubed potatoes, 2 crushed garlic cloves, ¼ cup chopped fresh cilantro leaves, 2½ cups hot vegetable broth, and 2 cups milk into a saucepan. Bring to a boil and cook for 5–6 minutes or until piping hot. Season and serve immediately.
Total cooking time 10 minutes.

walnut, gorgonzola & pear boats

Serves **4**

Total cooking time **10 minutes**

1 **ripe pear**, cored and finely
  chopped
2 tablespoons **crème fraîche**
  or **sour cream**
½ cup crumbled **Gorgonzola**
  or other **blue cheese**
20 **red** or **green Belgian
  endive leaves** (or a mixture
  of both)
¼ cup **walnuts**, toasted and
  coarsely chopped
olive oil, to drizzle

Mix together the pear, crème fraîche or sour cream,
and Gorgonzola or other blue cheese in a small bowl.

Arrange the endive leaves on a serving plate and spoon
a little of the pear mixture onto the bottom of each leaf.

Sprinkle the chopped nuts over the top of the filling,
drizzle with a little olive oil, and serve.

For baked endive & gorgonzola, trim any coarse
or bruised outer leaves from 8 large heads red endive.
Place in a baking dish into which they will fit snugly in
a single layer. Drizzle with ⅓ cup olive oil and season.
Sprinkle with ⅔ cup crumbled Gorgonzola or other blue
cheese and the juice of 1 lemon. Bake in a preheated
oven, at 350°F, for 20 minutes. Serve straight from the
baking dish with the juices and sprinkle with ¼ cup
chopped toasted walnuts before serving. **Total cooking
time 30 minutes.**

bean & red pepper bruschetta

Serves **4**

Total cooking time **20 minutes**

1 large **baguette**, cut into
   8 slices
3 tablespoons **olive oil**
1 **garlic clove**
1 (15 oz) **can cranberry
   beans**, rinsed and drained
3 **scallions**, sliced
½ cup drained and finely
   sliced **roasted red peppers**
   from a jar
6 **basil leaves**, thinly shredded
salt and **black pepper**

Place the slices of baguette on a baking sheet and drizzle with 2 tablespoons of the olive oil. Cook under a preheated hot broiler for 2–3 minutes on each side, until toasted and golden.

Rub each slice of toast with the garlic clove.

Place the drained cranberry beans and scallions in a bowl and lightly crush together with a fork.

Stir in the roasted red pepper, basil, remaining olive oil, and some salt and black pepper.

Spoon the bean mixture onto the toasted baguette slices and serve immediately.

For quick bean salad, in a large serving bowl, mix together 1 (15 oz) can cranberry beans, rinsed and drained, 3 sliced scallions, ½ cup drained and chopped roasted red peppers from a jar, 3 chopped tomatoes, 4–5 shredded basil leaves, 2 tablespoons olive oil, and 1 tablespoon balsamic vinegar. **Total cooking time 10 minutes.**

red pepper dip with herbed pitas

Serves **4**
Total cooking time **20 minutes**

⅓ cup **olive oil**
1 **shallot**, finely chopped
1 cup **walnut halves**
1 cup **roasted red peppers**
  from a jar
1 **garlic clove**, crushed
1 teaspoon **ground cumin**
1 tablespoon **pomegranate molasses**
4 **pita breads**
handful of chopped **parsley**
handful of chopped **mint**
kosher sea salt

Heat 1 tablespoon of the oil in a skillet, add the shallot, and cook for 3 minutes, until softened. Let cool.

Toast the walnut halves in a dry skillet for 3 minutes, until lightly browned, and let cool. Put the walnuts into a food processor with the shallot, roasted red peppers, garlic, cumin, pomegranate molasses, and 2 tablespoons of the oil and process together until smooth. Season.

Meanwhile, cut the pitas open horizontally and cut each half into wedges. Mix together the remaining oil with the herbs and brush over the wedges. Put onto a baking sheet, sprinkle with kosher sea salt, and bake in a preheated oven, at 375°F, for 5–7 minutes or until golden and crisp. Serve alongside the red pepper dip.

For herb & roasted pepper salad, lightly toast ¼ cup walnut halves in a dry skillet. Whisk 1 tablespoon sherry vinegar with 3 tablespoons olive oil. Toss with 5 cups mixed herbs and lettuce and 2 roasted red peppers, cut into strips, from a jar. Season to taste. Arrange on a plate, then sprinkle with the walnuts and 2 oz crumbled soft goat cheese. **Total cooking time 10 minutes.**

baked brie with maple syrup

Serves **4**

Total cooking time **20 minutes**

10 oz **whole baby Brie** or
  Camembert

¼ cup **pecans**

3 tablespoons **maple syrup**

3 tablespoons packed
  dark brown sugar

thyme sprigs

crusty bread, to serve

Remove any plastic packaging from the cheese and return it to its wooden box. Place on a baking sheet and cook in a preheated oven, at 400°F, for 15 minutes.

Meanwhile, toast the pecans in a small skillet for 3–5 minutes, until lightly browned, then set aside. Put the maple syrup and sugar into a small saucepan and bring to a boil. Cook for 1 minute until foamy.

Remove the cheese from the oven and cut a small cross in the center. Drizzle with the maple syrup, sprinkle with the pecans and thyme, and serve with plenty of crusty bread.

For brie salad with maple dressing, whisk together 1 tablespoon maple syrup with 1 teaspoon mustard, 1 tablespoon white wine vinegar, and 3 tablespoons olive oil. Season and toss together with 7 cups mixed salad greens. Arrange on plates with ¼ cup toasted pecans. Cut 4 oz Brie into thick slices. Put the Brie onto a baking sheet and cook under a hot broiler for 1 minute or until starting to melt. Dot it over the salad to serve. **Total cooking time 10 minutes.**

fava bean & pea crostini

Serves **6**
Total cooking time **20 minutes**

⅓ cup **olive oil**
1 **lemon**
2 **garlic cloves**, peeled
2 cups **fava beans**
2 cups **peas**
handful of **mint**
6 slices of **sourdough bread**
salt and **black pepper**

To serve
2 **radishes**, thinly sliced
handful of **pea shoots**
Pecorino cheese shavings

Put the oil, 3 strips of lemon zest, and the garlic cloves into a small saucepan and cook over low heat for 7–10 minutes. Remove from the heat and discard the lemon zest.

Cook the fava beans and peas in a saucepan of lightly salted boiling water for 3 minutes, until just soft. Drain and rinse under cold running water to cool. Peel the fava beans and discard the shells.

Transfer most of the peas and beans to a food processor, add the mint and cooked garlic together with the flavored oil, and pulse to make a coarse puree. Season well.

Toast the bread, halve the slices, and arrange on a serving plate. Spread with the puree and sprinkle with the reserved peas and fava beans. Top with radishes, pea shoots, and Pecorino cheese shavings and serve.

For pea & fava bean salad, cook ⅔ cup each of peas and fava beans in lightly salted boiling water for 3 minutes, until soft, then drain and cool under cold running water. Whisk 3 tablespoons olive oil with 1 tablespoon lemon juice, season, and toss with 5 cups salad greens. Place on serving plates, sprinkle with the peas and beans, and top with Pecorino cheese shavings to serve. **Total cooking time 10 minutes.**

asparagus with poached eggs

Serves **4**
Total cooking time **10 minutes**

1 ½ lb **asparagus spears**
1 tablespoon **olive oil**
4 **eggs**
2 oz **Parmesan cheese**

Snap the woody ends off the asparagus spears and discard. Heat a ridged grill pan until hot and sprinkle it with the oil.

Meanwhile, bring a skillet of water to a boil for the eggs.

Put the asparagus spears onto the grill pan and cook, turning regularly, until slightly charred at the ends.

Stir the boiling water vigorously, then, one at a time, drop the cracked eggs into the center—the swirling water will help the egg white collect around the yolk and maintain the shape of the egg. Cook for 4–5 minutes, then remove with a slotted spoon.

Serve the asparagus on 4 warm plates, and top with the poached eggs.

Using a vegetable peeler, make curly shavings of Parmesan and sprinkle on top of the asparagus.

For asparagus omelet, heat 1 tablespoon oil in a skillet, add 6 chopped asparagus spears, 2 sliced scallions, and 3–4 sliced cremini mushrooms, and cook for 5–6 minutes. Whisk together 5 eggs and ¼ cup milk and pour into the skillet, tipping the pan and moving the egg with a spatula to be sure it all cooks. Sprinkle with ¼ cup grated Parmesan, then put under a preheated hot broiler for 1–2 minutes, until golden. Cut into quarters and serve with a green salad and new potatoes. **Total cooking time 20 minutes.**

chickpea & spinach omelet

Serves **4**
Total cooking time **20 minutes**

2 tablespoons **olive oil**
1 large **onion**, sliced
1 **red bell pepper**, cored,
  seeded, and sliced
½ teaspoon **hot smoked** or
  sweet paprika
1 (15 oz) **can chickpeas
  (garbanzo beans)**, drained
  and rinsed
3½ cups **fresh spinach**,
  rinsed and coarsely sliced
5 **eggs**, lightly beaten
¾ cup **pitted green olives**,
  coarsely chopped
1¼ cups shredded
  cheddar cheese
salt and **black pepper**

Heat the olive oil in a large, nonstick skillet. Add the onion and bell pepper and cook gently for 7–8 minutes, until soft and golden. Stir in the paprika and chickpeas (garbanzo beans), and cook for 1 minute, stirring frequently. Add the spinach and cook until just wilted.

Pour the beaten eggs into the pan and stir to combine. Cook gently, without stirring, for 4–5 minutes, until almost set.

Sprinkle with the olives and shredded cheddar, then slide under a hot broiler, keeping the handle away from the heat. Broil for 4–5 minutes, until golden and set. Slice into wedges and serve immediately.

For chickpea & spinach salad with poached eggs,

heat 2 tablespoons olive oil in a large skillet. Add 1 sliced onion and 1 seeded and sliced red bell pepper, and cook gently for 7–8 minutes. Stir in ½ teaspoon hot smoked or sweet paprika and 1 (15 oz) can chickpeas (garbanzo beans), drained and rinsed, and cook for 1 minute, stirring frequently. Meanwhile, poach 4 eggs in a large saucepan of gently simmering water. Toss the chickpea mixture briefly with 1 (6 oz) package baby spinach and pile onto 4 serving plates. Top each salad with a poached egg and serve immediately. **Total cooking time 10 minutes.**

bean burgers with garlicky yogurt

Serves **4**
Total cooking time **30 minutes**

3 tablespoons **vegetable oil**
1 **onion**, finely chopped
1 **garlic clove**, chopped
1 (15 oz) **can kidney beans**,
  drained and rinsed
1 (15 oz) **can black-eyed
  peas**, drained and rinsed
1 tablespoon **tomato paste**
1 teaspoon **paprika** (optional)
¼ cup finely chopped
  flat leaf parsley
1 medium **egg**, lightly beaten
2 cups **fresh white bread
  crumbs**
1 cup **plain yogurt**
1 small **garlic clove**, crushed
2 teaspoons **lemon juice**
salt and **black pepper**
4 **soft flour tortillas**, warmed,
  to serve
lettuce, to garnish

Heat 2 tablespoons of the oil in a small skillet and cook the onion gently for 6–7 minutes. Add the chopped garlic and cook for an additional 2–3 minutes, until soft and golden.

Meanwhile, put the kidney beans and black-eyed peas into the large bowl of a food processor with the tomato paste, paprika, if using, and half the parsley. Pulse until the mixture becomes a coarse paste. Transfer to a bowl and add the egg, bread crumbs, and cooked onion mixture. Season with salt and black pepper, then mix well and shape into 4 large patties.

Heat the remaining oil in a large, nonstick skillet and cook the burgers gently for 8–10 minutes, turning once, until crisp and golden.

Meanwhile, mix the yogurt with the crushed garlic, the remaining parsley, and the lemon juice. Season with salt and black pepper and set aside.

Serve the burgers with warmed tortillas and the yogurt and garnish with lettuce.

For mixed bean hummus, put 2 cups rinsed and drained, canned mixed beans, such as kidney beans, pinto beans, and checkpeas (garbanzo beans) into a food processor with 1 tablespoon tomato paste, 1 teaspoon paprika, ¼ cup finely chopped flat leaf parsley, 1 small crushed garlic clove, and 2 teaspoons lemon juice, and blend to a paste. Add enough yogurt to give a smooth, creamy consistency, then season and serve with a selection of raw vegetables for dipping. **Total cooking time 10 minutes.**

feta-stuffed sweet peppers

Serves **4**

Total cooking time **20 minutes**

1 tablespoon **olive oil**

4 **long sweet peppers**

2 **egg yolks**

1⅓ cups crumbled
  feta cheese

3 tablespoons **plain yogurt**

finely grated zest of ½ **lemon**

1 teaspoon chopped **oregano**

Rub the oil over the sweet peppers, arrange them in a broiler pan, and cook under a preheated hot broiler for 5 minutes, turning once, until just soft. Let cool for a couple of minutes, then cut in half lengthwise and remove the seeds.

Put the egg yolks, 1 cup of the feta, the yogurt, and lemon zest into a food processor and blend until smooth. Spoon the mixture into the sweet peppers, then sprinkle the remaining feta on top along with the oregano.

Return to the broiler and cook for 5–7 minutes, until golden and cooked through. Let set for a couple of minutes before serving.

For spicy baked feta with roasted peppers, lightly grease 4 large sheets of aluminum foil. Divide 1 thinly sliced red onion between the sheets and top with 2 chopped roasted red peppers and a handful of halved cherry tomatoes. Put a 4 oz chunk of feta cheese on top of each portion and divide a handful of chopped oregano and 1 sliced red chile among them. Drizzle with a little olive oil, then fold up the foil to make airtight packages. Place on a baking sheet and cook in a preheated oven, at 400°F, for 20 minutes. Serve with plenty of crusty bread. **Total cooking time 30 minutes.**

ciabatta toast with broiled veggies

Serves **4**

Total cooking time **10 minutes**

⅓ cup **olive oil**, plus extra
for drizzling
½ **eggplant**, trimmed and
thinly sliced
1 **ciabatta loaf**
¼ cup **green pesto**
1 large **beefsteak tomato**,
thinly sliced
4 slices of **mozzarella cheese**
black pepper

Heat the oil in a large, heavy skillet and cook the eggplant slices, in batches, over high heat for 1–2 minutes on each side, until browned and tender. Remove with a spatula and keep warm.

Meanwhile, cut the ciabatta loaf in half lengthwise, then each half in half again widthwise. Put onto the broiler rack and cook under a preheated high broiler, cut side up, for 1 minute, until golden.

Spread each ciabatta toast with 1 tablespoon of the pesto. Top with the warm eggplant slices, followed by the tomato slices, and, finally, the mozzarella slices. Drizzle each toast with 1 tablespoon olive oil, then return to the broiler and cook for an additional 2 minutes, until the mozzarella is melting and beginning to brown.

Season with black pepper and serve warm.

For Mediterranean vegetable gratin, gently heat ¼ cup olive oil in a large skillet and cook 1 sliced eggplant, in batches, over high heat for 1–2 minutes on each side, until browned and tender. Loosely layer in a large, shallow gratin dish with 3 sliced beefsteak tomatoes, 10 oz sliced mozzarella cheese, and ⅓ cup green pesto, seasoning between the layers. Sprinkle with 3 tablespoons freshly grated Parmesan cheese and cook under a preheated high broiler for 8–10 minutes, until golden and bubbling. **Total cooking time 30 minutes.**

soups & salads

lettuce, pea & tarragon soup

Serves **4**
Total cooking time **20 minutes**

2 tablespoons **butter**
8 **scallions**, trimmed
and sliced
5 cups **frozen peas**
(about 1½ lb)
1 tablespoon chopped
tarragon
1 **romaine lettuce**, finely
shredded
4 cups **hot vegetable broth**
2 tablespoons **heavy cream**
salt and **black pepper**
tarragon sprigs, to garnish
(optional)

Melt the butter in a large saucepan over medium heat. Add the scallions and cook, stirring continuously, for 2 minutes.

Stir in the peas, half the tarragon, and the lettuce. Cook for 1 minute.

Add the broth, bring to a boil, cover, and simmer for 5 minutes or until tender.

Pour the soup into a blender, add the remaining tarragon, and blend until smooth. Season.

Divide the soup among 4 bowls, swirl the cream into each bowl, and sprinkle with black pepper. Garnish with tarragon sprigs, if desired.

For lettuce, pea, tomato & scallion salad, separate the leaves of 2 washed romaine lettuce and put into a large, wide salad bowl with 8 sliced scallions, 4 sliced plum tomatoes, 3⅓ cups (1 lb) blanched peas, and 12 sliced radishes. Make a dressing by whisking together the juice of 1 lemon, ⅓ cup olive oil, 1 teaspoon Dijon mustard, 2 tablespoons finely chopped tarragon, and 2 teaspoons honey. Season and pour the dressing over the salad ingredients. Toss to mix well and serve. **Total cooking time 10 minutes.**

roasted tomato soup

Serves **4**
Total cooking time **30 minutes**

8 **ripe tomatoes** (about 2 lb),
   halved
4 **garlic cloves**, unpeeled
2 tablespoons **olive oil**
1 **onion**, chopped
1 **carrot**, chopped
1 **celery stick**, sliced
1 **red bell pepper**, cored,
   seeded, and chopped
3 cups **hot vegetable broth**
salt and **black pepper**
¼ cup grated **Parmesan
   cheese**, to serve

Put the tomato halves and garlic cloves into a roasting pan. Sprinkle with 1 tablespoon of the olive oil and some black pepper and roast in a preheated oven, at 400°F, for 20 minutes.

After 10 minutes, heat the remaining olive oil in a saucepan and sauté the onion, carrot, celery, and red bell pepper over low heat for 10 minutes.

When the tomatoes are cooked, remove the garlic cloves in their skins and squeeze the garlic flesh into the pan with the sautéed vegetables.

Pour in the roast tomatoes and all the juices along with the broth. Using an immersion blender, or in a food processor or blender, blend the soup until smooth. Season.

Reheat, if necessary, then serve sprinkled with the grated Parmesan.

For quick tomato soup, heat 2 tablespoons olive oil in a saucepan and sauté 1 chopped onion, 1 chopped carrot, 1 chopped celery stick, and 6 chopped tomatoes (about 1½ lb) for 5 minutes. Pour in 1 (14½ oz) can diced tomatoes and 4 cups hot vegetable broth. Simmer for 10 minutes, remove from the heat, and add a small handful of basil. Using an immersion blender, or in a food processor or blender, blend the soup until smooth. Season to taste and serve with an extra drizzle of olive oil. **Total cooking time 20 minutes.**

asian soup with egg & greens

Serves **4**

Total cooking time **30 minutes**

4 **scallions**

1½ cups coarsely chopped
   bok choy

2 tablespoons **vegetable oil**

1 inch piece **fresh ginger
   root**, finely grated

2 **garlic cloves**, finely chopped

1 cup **jasmine rice**

½ cup **rice wine**

2 tablespoons **soy sauce**

1 teaspoon **rice wine vinegar**

4 cups **hot vegetable broth**

4 **eggs**

1 tablespoon **chili oil**,
   for drizzling

Finely slice the scallions, keeping the white and green parts separate. Combine the green parts with the bok choy in a bowl and set aside.

Heat the oil gently in a saucepan. When hot, add the scallion whites, ginger, and garlic and stir-fry for 2–3 minutes.

Add the rice, stir, then add the wine and simmer for a minute or so.

Add the soy sauce, vinegar, and broth and simmer, stirring occasionally, for 10–12 minutes. Then stir in the reserved scallions and bok choy and cook for an additional 2–3 minutes. Meanwhile, poach the eggs in two batches.

To serve, ladle the soup into 4 shallow soup bowls and top each one with a poached egg and drizzle with the chili oil.

For Asian rice & green salad, put ¼ head blanched and coarsely chopped bok choy into a salad bowl with 6 sliced scallions and 2½ cups cooked jasmine rice. Make a dressing by whisking together 1 crushed garlic clove, 1 teaspoon grated ginger, ¼ teaspoon chili oil, 2 tablespoons light soy sauce, the juice of 2 limes, a dash of rice wine vinegar, and ¼ cup vegetable oil. Season, pour the dressing over the salad, and toss to mix well before serving.
Total cooking time 10 minutes

sweet potato & red pepper soup

Serves **4**

Total cooking time **20 minutes**

2 tablespoons **vegetable oil**

1 **red onion**, chopped

1 **red bell pepper**, cored,
   seeded, and chopped

3 **sweet potatoes** (about 1 lb),
   peeled and chopped

¼ teaspoon **ground cumin**

8 **cherry tomatoes**

5 cups **vegetable broth**

⅓ cup **flaked dried coconut**

salt and **black pepper**

To serve

plain yogurt

fresh cilantro sprigs

Heat the oil in a saucepan over medium heat, add the onion and bell pepper, and cook for 3–4 minutes. Stir in the sweet potatoes, cumin, and tomatoes, and cook for an additional 2–3 minutes.

Pour in the broth, bring to a boil, and simmer for 12 minutes. Stir in the coconut and cook for an additional 2–3 minutes. Using an immersion blender or food processor, blend the soup until smooth.

Season with salt and black pepper and serve topped with a dollop of plain yogurt and a sprig of cilantro.

For warm sweet potato wedges salad, slice 5 sweet potatoes (about 1¾ lb) into wedges. In a large bowl, mix together 2 crushed garlic cloves, ¼ cup olive oil, 2 teaspoons chopped sage, 1 teaspoon paprika, and some salt and black pepper. Toss the potato in the herb and spice mixture, put into a roasting pan, and roast in a preheated oven, at 400°F, for 25 minutes. Serve the potato wedges tossed with 1 (6 oz) package baby spinach and 4 chopped scallions. **Total cooking time 30 minutes.**

lentil, mustard & chickpea soup

Serves **4**

Total cooking time **20 minutes**

½ teaspoon **coconut oil** or
   olive oil

¼ teaspoon **mustard seeds**

½ teaspoon **ground cumin**

½ teaspoon **ground turmeric**

1 small **onion**, diced

¾-inch piece of **fresh ginger
   root**, finely chopped

1 **garlic clove**, finely chopped

½ cup **red split lentils**

1 cup rinsed and drained,
   **canned chickpeas
   (garbanzo beans)**

4 cups **hot vegetable broth**

2 cups **baby spinach**

salt and **black pepper**

Heat the oil in a saucepan and add the dry spices.
When the mustard seeds start to pop, add the onion,
ginger, and garlic and cook until the onion softens.

Add the lentils and chickpeas (garbanzo beans) and
stir well to coat. Pour in the broth and bring to a boil,
then reduce the heat and simmer for 14–16 minutes,
until the lentils are cooked.

Stir in the spinach until wilted, then season. Ladle the
soup into bowls and serve.

For lentil & chickpea salad with warm mustard
dressing, heat 3 tablespoons olive oil in a large skillet,
add 1 seeded and chopped red chile, ½ teaspoon
mustard seeds, 2 sliced garlic cloves, and a 1-inch
piece of peeled and grated ginger root, and sauté
for 2 minutes. Remove from the heat and stir in
1 small sliced red onion, 2 cups cooled, cooked lentils,
1 (15 oz) can chickpeas (garbanzo beans), rinsed
and drained, the juice of ½ lemon, and 2 tablespoons
chopped sun-dried tomatoes. Stir together, pour
into a serving bowl, and toss with 2 cups arugula
and 1 cup crumbled feta cheese. **Total cooking
time 10 minutes.**

iced green gazpacho

Total preparation time
20 minutes

2 **celery sticks** (including
  leaves)
1 small **green bell pepper**,
  seeded
1 large **cucumber**, peeled
3 slices **stale white bread**,
  crusts removed
1 **fresh green chile**, seeded
4 **garlic cloves**
1 teaspoon **honey**
1½ cups **walnuts**, lightly
  toasted
1 (6 oz) package
  baby spinach
2 cups **basil**
¼ cup **apple cider vinegar**
1 cup **extra virgin olive oil**,
  plus extra for drizzling
⅓ cup **plain yogurt**
2 cups **iced water**
handful of **ice cubes**
salt and **black pepper**
store-bought croutons,
  to serve

Chop coarsely the celery, bell pepper, cucumber, bread, chile, and garlic.

Put into a blender and add the honey, walnuts, spinach, basil, vinegar, oil, yogurt, most of the iced water, and the ice cubes, and season well. Blend the soup until smooth. Add more iced water, if needed, to achieve the desired consistency.

Taste the soup and adjust the seasoning, if necessary.

Serve in chilled bowls and garnish with croutons and a drizzle of olive oil.

For green vegetable salad, put 4 thinly sliced celery sticks, 1 sliced cucumber, 1 seeded and thinly sliced green bell pepper, and 3½ cups baby spinach into a large, wide bowl. Make a dressing by whisking ⅔ cup plain yogurt in a bowl with the juice of 1 lime, 1 crushed garlic clove, 1 teaspoon honey, and 1 finely diced green chile. Drizzle the dressing over the salad and sprinkle with a small handful of store-bought croutons before serving. **Total cooking time 10 minutes.**

spicy lentil & carrot soup

Serves **4**
Total cooking time **30 minutes**

2 tablespoons **sunflower oil**
1 **garlic clove**, finely chopped
1 teaspoon grated **fresh
   ginger root**
1 **red chile**, finely chopped
1 **onion**, finely chopped
1 tablespoon **sweet smoked
   paprika**, plus extra to garnish
12 **carrots** (about 1½ lb),
   peeled and finely chopped
¾ cup **red split lentils**, rinsed
   and drained
⅔ cup **light cream**
4 cups **hot vegetable broth**
½ cup **crème fraîche** or
   sour cream
small handful of chopped **fresh
   cilantro leaves**
salt and **black pepper**

Caramelized onions
1 tablespoon **butter**
1 tablespoon **olive oil**
1 **onion**, thinly sliced

Heat the sunflower oil in a heavy saucepan, add the garlic, ginger, red chile, onion, and smoked paprika, and cook, stirring, over medium-high heat for 1–2 minutes. Add the carrots, lentils, cream, and broth and bring to a boil, then reduce the heat to medium and simmer, uncovered, for 15–20 minutes.

Meanwhile, to make the caramelized onions, heat the butter and olive oil in a skillet, add the onion, and cook over low heat for 12–15 minutes or until caramelized and golden brown. Drain on paper towels and keep warm.

Using an immersion blender or food processor, blend the lentil mixture in the pan until smooth, then season well.

Ladle into bowls, add a dollop of crème fraiche or sour cream, and sprinkle with chopped cilantro leaves and the caramelized onions. Sprinkle with a little smoked paprika before serving.

For spicy lentil & carrot salad, put 4 cups cooled, cooked green lentils, 2 peeled and shredded carrots, 1 finely chopped red chile, 4 sliced scallions, and a large handful of chopped fresh cilantro leaves into a salad bowl. Pour ⅔ cup store-bought French salad dressing over the salad and add 1 teaspoon sweet smoked paprika. Season, toss to mix, and serve. **Total cooking time 10 minutes.**

tuscan bean & truffle soup

Serves **4**

Total cooking time **20 minutes**

2 tablespoons **olive oil**

1 **onion**, chopped

2 **garlic cloves**, sliced

1 (15 oz) **can cannellini (white kidney) beans**, rinsed and drained

1 (15 oz) **can lima beans**, rinsed and drained

1 (14½ oz) **can diced tomatoes**

½ head **savoy cabbage**, shredded

1½ teaspoons chopped **rosemary**

3½ cups **vegetable broth**

1 teaspoon **truffle oil**

salt and **black pepper**

¼ cup grated **Parmesan cheese**, to serve

Heat the oil in a saucepan over medium heat, add the onion, and cook for 1–2 minutes, until softened.

Stir the garlic, cannellini (white kidney) beans, and lima beans into the onions and cook for 1 minute.

Add the tomatoes, cabbage, and rosemary to the pan, then pour in the broth and the truffle oil. Mix together well, season, and bring to a boil. Simmer for 10–12 minutes, until the cabbage is just cooked.

Divide the soup among 4 shallow dishes and sprinkle with the Parmesan to serve.

For tuscan bean & truffle salad, steam 1½ cups trimmed green beans for 2–3 minutes, then refresh under cold running water and toss together with 1 (15 oz) can each of cannellini (white kidney) beans and lima beans, rinsed and drained, 1 cup halved baby tomatoes, 4 sliced scallions, and 2 tablespoons chopped parsley. Whisk together 3 tablespoons olive oil, 2 teaspoons truffle oil, 1 tablespoon balsamic vinegar, and 1 teaspoon honey, pour the dressing over the salad, and toss to serve. **Total cooking time 10 minutes.**

beet & goat cheese salad

Serves **4**

Total cooking time **10 minutes**

2 tablespoons **olive oil**

3 **raw beets**, peeled and
    grated

¼ cup **balsamic vinegar**

2 tablespoons **sunflower
    seeds**

7 oz **goat cheese**

3 cups **arugula**

2 tablespoons **extra virgin
    olive oil**

black pepper

Heat the olive oil in a skillet, add the beets, and cook for 3–4 minutes. Season well with black pepper, then stir in the vinegar and cook over high heat for 30 seconds.

Meanwhile, heat a nonstick skillet over medium-low heat and dry-fry the sunflower seeds for 2 minutes, stirring frequently, until golden and toasted. Set aside.

Divide the beets among 4 plates. Crumble the cheese over them and top with the arugula.

Serve drizzled with the extra virgin olive oil and sprinkled with the toasted sunflower seeds.

For beet soup with goat cheese, heat 1 tablespoon olive oil in a saucepan, add 1 chopped onion, and cook for 2–3 minutes. Add 3 grated raw beets, 2½ cups hot vegetable broth, and 1 (14½ oz) can diced tomatoes and bring to a boil. Reduce the heat and simmer for 8–10 minutes, until the beets are tender. Using an immersion blender or food processor, blend the soup until smooth, then season. Ladle into bowls and crumble 4 oz goat cheese over the top before serving. **Total cooking time 20 minutes.**

cream of squash & apple soup

Serves **4**
Total cooking time **30 minutes**

2 tablespoons **olive oil**
1 **onion**, chopped
1 small **butternut squash**
    or 1 medium **acorn squash**
    (about 1½ lb), peeled,
    seeded, and cut into chunks
1 **Granny Smith apple**,
    peeled, cored, and chopped
2 **tomatoes**, skinned and
    chopped
4 cups **vegetable broth**
½ cup **heavy cream**
1 tablespoon finely chopped
    flat leaf parsley
salt and **black pepper**

Heat the olive oil in a large saucepan and sauté the onion for 3–4 minutes.

Add the squash and stir to coat with the onion. Stir in the apple and the chopped tomatoes.

Pour in the broth, bring to a boil, and then simmer, covered, for 20 minutes, until the squash is tender.

Let the soup cool a little before pouring in the cream. Using an immersion blender, or in a food processor or blender, blend the soup until smooth.

Gently reheat, if necessary, season, and serve immediately, sprinkled with chopped parsley.

For squash & chickpea salad, peel, seed, and dice 1 butternut squash (about 2 lb). Toss with 1 crushed garlic clove, ½ teaspoon ground cumin, and 2 tablespoons olive oil and roast in a preheated oven, at 400°F, for 15 minutes. Mix the roasted squash with 1 (15 oz) can chickpeas (garbanzo beans), rinsed and drained, 1 small diced red onion, 1 cup crumbled feta cheese, ½ cup drained sun-dried tomatoes in oil, and 2 cups arugula. Serve dressed with store-bought Italian salad dressing. **Total cooking time 20 minutes.**

watermelon & halloumi salad

Serves **4**
Total cooking time **10 minutes**

8 oz **halloumi** or **Muenster
    cheese**, cut into 8 slices
finely grated zest and juice
    of **1 lime**
2 **scallions**, finely sliced
2 tablespoons chopped **flat
    leaf parsley**
2 tablespoons chopped **mint**
1 tablespoon **avocado oil**
1 (5 oz) package **arugula**
½ **small watermelon**, peeled,
    seeded, and diced
½ small **red onion**, finely
    sliced
1 cup **almond-stuffed
    green olives**
1 tablespoon **pomegranate
    molasses**
1–2 teaspoons **chili paste**,
    to taste
½ cup **pomegranate seeds**
    (about 1 pomegranate)
black pepper

Preheat the broiler. Toss the cheese with the lime zest, scallions, and 1 tablespoon each of the parsley and mint, then put onto an aluminum foil-lined baking sheet. Drizzle with a little of the avocado oil and place it under the broiler for 3–4 minutes, until hot and golden, turning once.

Meanwhile, arrange the arugula on 4 large plates. Toss the watermelon, onion, olives, and remaining parsley and mint in a large bowl. Spoon the dressed watermelon over the arugula.

In a small bowl, mix together the lime juice, pomegranate molasses, the remaining avocado oil, and chili paste, to taste, then season with black pepper.

Top each salad with 2 slices of the broiled cheese, then sprinkle with the pomegranate seeds. Serve drizzled with the dressing.

For watermelon & feta salad, peel, seed, and dice ½ small watermelon and arrange on serving plates. Crumble 7 oz feta over the watermelon, then sprinkle with 2 finely sliced scallions, 2 tablespoons each of chopped mint and parsley, and 1 cup black ripe olives. Sprinkle with ½ cup pomegranate seeds and serve drizzled with 1 tablespoon pomegranate molasses. **Total cooking time 10 minutes.**

spicy soybean & noodle salad

Serves **4**
Total cooking time **15 minutes**

8 oz **dried soba noodles**
1 ½ cups **frozen shelled soybeans**
6 **scallions**, thinly sliced diagonally
2 tablespoons **sesame seeds**
1 inch piece of **fresh ginger root**
1 **red chile,** finely chopped
1 tablespoon **toasted sesame oil**
3 tablespoons **mirin**
3 tablespoons **light soy sauce**
1 teaspoon **honey**
salt
chopped **fresh cilantro leaves**, to garnish

Cook the noodles and soybeans in a large saucepan of lightly salted boiling water for 4–5 minutes, or according to the noodle package directions. Drain well, then return to the pan and add the scallions. Cover and keep warm.

Heat a skillet until hot, add the sesame seeds, and dry-fry over medium heat until lightly golden, then remove from the pan and set aside.

Peel and grate the ginger root into a bowl, then stir in the remaining ingredients and mix well. Pour the dressing over the noodle mixture and toss to mix well.

Ladle into warm bowls, sprinkle with the sesame seeds and chopped cilantro, and serve.

For spicy soybean, ginger & noodle broth, put 3 ½ cups hot vegetable broth, 1 teaspoon peeled and grated fresh ginger root, 1 chopped red chile, and 6 finely sliced scallions into a saucepan and bring to a boil, then add 12 oz cooked soba noodles and 1 ½ cups frozen shelled soybeans. Bring back to a boil, then season and serve sprinkled with chopped fresh cilantro leaves and a drizzle of sesame oil. **Total cooking time 10 minutes.**

bulgur & goat cheese salad

Serves **4**

Total cooking time **20 minutes**

3 cups **hot vegetable broth**
2 cups **bulgur**
¼ cup **olive** or **vegetable oil**
1 large **red onion**, halved
    and thinly sliced
½ cup **tomato juice**
2 tablespoons **lime juice**
6 oz **firm goat cheese**,
    crumbled
3 tablespoons coarsely
    chopped **flat leaf parsley**
salt and **black pepper**

Bring the vegetable broth to a boil in a large saucepan, add the bulgur, and cook for 7 minutes. Remove from the heat, cover with a tight-fitting lid, and set aside for 5–8 minutes, until the liquid has been absorbed and the grains are tender.

Meanwhile, heat 2 tablespoons of oil in a skillet and cook the onion gently for 7–8 minutes, until soft and golden.

Combine the remaining oil with the tomato juice and lime juice, and season with salt and black pepper. Fold the dressing, onion, goat cheese, and parsley into the bulgur with a fork, and spoon into 4 shallow bowls to serve.

For goat cheese couscous, put 1½ cups couscous into a bowl with 1 tablespoon of olive or vegetable oil and a generous pinch of salt. Pour 1¼ cups boiling vegetable broth over the bulgur and set aside for 5–8 minutes, until the grains are tender and the liquid has been absorbed. Meanwhile, combine 3 tablespoons oil with ½ cup tomato juice and 2 tablespoons lime juice, and season with salt and black pepper. Fold the goat cheese and parsley into the couscous and spoon into serving bowls. Drizzle with the dressing and sprinkle with 3 sliced scallions to serve. **Total cooking time 10 minutes.**

quinoa & tomato salad with feta

Serves **4**

Total cooking time **30 minutes**

1 cup **quinoa**, rinsed under
running cold water

1¼ cups **boiling water**

4 **yellow** or **red tomatoes**,
seeded and diced

1 large **green bell pepper**,
seeded and finely chopped

2 **scallions**, finely sliced

1 cup **pitted Kalamata olives**,
coarsely chopped

½ **cucumber**, cut in half
lengthwise, seeded,
and sliced

grated zest and juice of
1 **lemon**

3 tablespoons chopped **flat
leaf parsley**

3 tablespoons chopped **mint**

4 small **red** or **white endive**,
sliced

4 oz **feta cheese**

2 tablespoons **toasted
mixed seeds**

small handful of **alfalfa
sprouts**

salt and **black pepper**

lemon wedges, to serve

Put the quinoa into a medium saucepan and pour over the measured boiling water. Cover the pan and simmer gently for 12–15 minutes. It is ready when the seed begins to come away from the germ. Drain the quinoa in a fine-mesh strainer and cool under running cold water. Drain well.

Meanwhile, mix together in a large bowl the tomatoes, bell pepper, scallions, olives, and cucumber, then stir in the lemon zest, parsley, and mint.

Mix the cooled quinoa through the vegetables and season with salt, black pepper, and lemon juice, to taste. Set aside for 5–10 minutes to let the flavors develop.

Sprinkle the endive onto 4 serving plates, spoon over the quinoa salad, and crumble the feta over the top. Sprinkle with the toasted seeds and alfalfa sprouts and serve with the lemon wedges.

For minted pea quinoa, heat 1 (8 oz) package ready-to-eat red and white quinoa or ready-to-eat red mixed wholesome grains, according to the package directions. Transfer the quinoa or grains to a bowl and toss with 3 tablespoons each of chopped flat leaf parsley and mint, 1 cup thawed frozen peas, and 2 finely sliced scallions. Season with salt, black pepper, and lemon juice to taste. Sprinkle with 1 cup shredded cheddar cheese and 2 tablespoons toasted mixed seeds and serve. **Total cooking time 10 minutes.**

panzanella

Serves **4**
Total cooking time **30 minutes**

3 **ripe tomatoes**
1 **ciabatta roll** (about 4 oz)
16 **black ripe olives**, pitted
3 teaspoons **capers**
½ **red onion**, finely sliced
18 **red** and **yellow cherry tomatoes**, halved
6–8 **basil leaves**
1 tablespoon **red wine vinegar**
2 tablespoons **olive oil**

Put the tomatoes into a strainer over a bowl. Using the back of a spoon, squash them well to release all the juice into the bowl.

Coarsely break up the bread and add it to the tomato juice. Let stand for 15 minutes, then transfer to a serving dish.

Sprinkle the remaining ingredients over the soaked bread, drizzling it with the red wine vinegar and olive oil before serving.

For tomato salad with ciabatta croutons,
cut 1 ciabatta roll (about 4 oz) into cubes. Heat 2 tablespoons olive oil in a skillet and sauté the cubes of bread until they are golden. Drain on paper towels. Toss the fried bread together with 3 coarsely chopped ripe tomatoes, 16 pitted black ripe olives, ½ sliced red onion, 18 red and yellow cherry tomatoes, 6–8 torn basil leaves and 2 cups baby spinach. Drizzle with 2 tablespoons olive oil and 1 tablespoon red wine vinegar to serve. **Total cooking time 10 minutes.**

chickpea, tomato & pepper salad

Serves **4**
Total cooking time **30 minutes**

3 large **red bell peppers**,
    cored, seeded, and cut
    into quarters
6 **plum tomatoes**, halved
¼ cup **olive oil**
1 teaspoon **cumin seeds**
1 tablespoon **lemon juice**
½ teaspoon **Dijon mustard**
½ teaspoon **honey**
1 (15 oz) **can chickpeas**
    (garbanzo beans), drained
10–12 **basil leaves**, coarsely
    torn
3½ cups **baby spinach**
salt and **black pepper**

Put the bell peppers and tomatoes into a roasting pan and toss with 1 tablespoon of the oil and the cumin seeds. Season with salt and black pepper and roast in a preheated oven, at 425°F, for 20 minutes.

Whisk the remaining oil with the lemon juice, mustard, and honey to make a dressing.

Remove the bell peppers from the oven and transfer to a bowl. Stir in the chickpeas (garbanzo beans), basil, and spinach, pour the dressing over the salad, and serve immediately.

For chickpea, tomato & pepper soup, heat 1 tablespoon olive oil in a large saucepan over medium heat, add 1 seeded and chopped red bell pepper and 1 diced red onion, and cook for 1–2 minutes. Stir in 1 (15 oz) can of chickpeas (garbanzo beans), rinsed and drained, and 3 chopped plum tomatoes. Pour in 4 cups vegetable broth and season well. Simmer for 4–5 minutes. Using an immersion blender or food processor, blend until smooth and serve with a drizzle of olive oil. **Total cooking time 10 minutes.**

midweek meals

asparagus & pea quinoa risotto

Serves **4**

Total cooking time **20 minutes**

1⅔ cups **quinoa**, rinsed

2½ cups **hot vegetable broth**

8 oz **asparagus**, chopped

1⅓ cups **frozen peas**

1 tablespoon chopped **mint**

3 tablespoons grated
  Parmesan cheese

black pepper

Place the quinoa and broth into a saucepan and bring to a boil, then reduce the heat and simmer for 12–15 minutes, until the quinoa is cooked, adding the asparagus and peas about 2 minutes before the end of the cooking time.

Drain the quinoa and vegetables, then return to the pan with the mint and 2 tablespoons of the cheese and season with black pepper. Mix well.

Serve sprinkled with the remaining Parmesan.

For asparagus & pea tart, unroll a sheet of ready-to-bake puff pastry and place on a baking sheet. Mix together 1 cup cream cheese and 1 tablespoon Dijon mustard in a bowl, then spread over the pastry, leaving a ¾ inch border around the edge. Top with 8 oz trimmed asparagus and ⅔ cup defrosted peas. Drizzle with 2 tablespoons olive oil, then season with black pepper and sprinkle with ½ cup grated Parmesan cheese. Place in a preheated oven, at 400°F, for 20–22 minutes. Serve with a crisp green salad. **Total cooking time 30 minutes.**

crispy spinach & feta pie

Serves **4**
Total cooking time **30 minutes**

1 (10 oz) package
 frozen spinach
2 **scallions**, chopped
1 **garlic clove**, crushed
1⅓ cups crumbled **feta
 cheese**
2 **eggs**, beaten
pinch of **grated nutmeg**
2 tablespoons **butter**, melted
3 tablespoons **olive oil**
5 large **phyllo pastry sheets**
salt and **black pepper**

Put the spinach into a strainer, then pour over boiling water to defrost. Squeeze to remove excess water, then mix with the scallions, garlic, feta, and eggs. Add the nutmeg and season.

Stir together the butter and oil and brush over the sides and bottom of an 8 inch springform cake pan. Unwrap the phyllo pastry and cover with damp paper towels until ready to use it.

Working quickly, brush 1 sheet with the butter mixture and arrange in the pan, letting the excess pastry hang over the sides. Brush another sheet with the butter mixture, turn the pan a little, and arrange it in the same way. Repeat until the bottom and sides of the pan are completely covered.

Spoon the filling into the pan, then fold the pastry edges over to cover the filling, scrunching them up a little as you work. Brush the top of the pie with a little more butter mixture and cook in a preheated oven, at 400°F, for 20–25 minutes, until golden and crisp.

For spinach, feta & chickpea salad, whisk together 1 tablespoon lemon juice, 3 tablespoons olive oil, and a pinch of ground cumin. Toss with 1 (15 oz) can chickpeas (garbanzo beans), rinsed and drained, and ½ thinly sliced red onion and season well. Stir in 4 cups baby spinach and 1 chopped roasted red pepper and arrange on a serving plate. Sprinkle with ½ cup crumbled feta cheese and serve. **Total cooking time 10 minutes.**

quick spiced cauliflower pilaf

Serves **4**
Total cooking time **10 minutes**

3 tablespoons **raisins**
3 cups small **cauliflower florets**
2 tablespoons **vegetable oil**
2 **garlic cloves**, crushed
2 **scallions**, thinly sliced
1½ tablespoons **medium-hot curry paste**
2½ cups **cooked pilaf rice**
chopped **fresh cilantro leaves**, to garnish
flatbreads, to serve (optional)

Put the raisins into a heatproof bowl, pour in 2 tablespoons boiling water, and set aside to soak.

Cook the cauliflower florets in a large saucepan of boiling water for 4–5 minutes, until just tender.

Meanwhile, heat the oil in a large saucepan and sauté the garlic and scallions over medium heat for 1 minute to soften. Add the curry paste and stir for 1 minute to cook the spices. Add the steamed rice and the raisins and their water, then cover and cook over medium-low heat for 2–3 minutes.

Drain the cauliflower and fold it into the rice. Spoon into dishes, garnish with the cilantro, and serve accompanied by flatbreads, if desired.

For aromatic spiced cauliflower stew, heat 2 tablespoons vegetable oil in a saucepan and cook 1 chopped onion, 2 chopped garlic cloves, and 1 teaspoon cumin seeds over medium heat for 6–7 minutes, stirring occasionally, until softened. Add 2 tablespoons medium-hot curry paste and stir for 1 minute. Add 5 cups cauliflower florets and 1 (15 oz) can rinsed and drained chickpeas (garbanzo beans) and stir. Pour in 1 (14½ oz) can plum tomatoes plus 1 cup water, then season, cover loosely, and simmer for 15–18 minutes, until tender. Serve sprinkled with chopped fresh cilantro leaves and a dollop of plain yogurt. **Total cooking time 30 minutes.**

94

ranch-style eggs

Serves **4**
Total cooking time **30 minutes**

2 tablespoons **olive oil**
1 **onion,** finely sliced
1 **red chile,** seeded and
    finely chopped
1 **garlic clove,** crushed
1 teaspoon **ground cumin**
1 teaspoon **dried oregano**
1 (14½ oz) **can cherry
    tomatoes**
1 cup drained and coarsely
    chopped **roasted red and
    yellow peppers in oil**
    from a jar
4 **eggs**
salt and **black pepper**
¼ cup finely chopped **fresh
    cilantro,** to garnish

Heat the oil in a large skillet and add the onion, chile, garlic, cumin, and oregano.

Sauté gently for about 5 minutes or until soft, then add the tomatoes and roasted peppers and cook for an additional 5 minutes. If the sauce looks dry, add a splash of water. Season well.

Make 4 hollows in the mixture, break an egg into each, and cover the pan. Cook for 5 minutes or until the eggs are just set.

Serve immediately, garnished with chopped cilantro.

For spicy Mexican-style scrambled eggs, heat 1 tablespoon each olive oil and butter in a large skillet. Whisk together 8 eggs with 1 crushed garlic clove, 1 finely chopped red chile, 1 teaspoon dried oregano, and 1 teaspoon ground cumin. Season, pour into the skillet, and cook over medium-low heat, stirring often or until the eggs are scrambled and cooked to your preference. Serve with warm tortillas and garnish with chopped fresh cilantro. **Total cooking time 10 minutes.**

potato gnocchi

Serves **4**
Total cooking time **30 minutes**

7 **russet** or **Yukon Gold
  potatoes** (about 1¾ lb),
  peeled and diced
1 **egg yolk**, beaten
1¼ cups **all-purpose flour**
⅓ cup finely shredded **basil**
½ cup grated **Parmesan
  cheese**
¼ cup **extra-virgin olive oil**
salt and **black pepper**

Cook the potatoes in a saucepan of boiling water for 12–15 minutes, until soft. Drain and mash, or use a potato ricer to get a really smooth texture. Put another saucepan of water on the heat to boil.

Transfer the mashed potatoes to a bowl and mix in the egg yolk, flour, and basil. Mix well to combine.

Take a teaspoon of the mixture into your hand and roll into a walnut-size ball. Press with the prongs of a fork to make a gnocchi shape. Repeat with the remaining mixture.

Drop the gnocchi into the saucepan of boiling water to cook; this should take only 1–2 minutes and the gnocchi will float when cooked.

Toss the hot gnocchi in the grated Parmesan and olive oil and serve immediately.

For potato gnocchi in a quick tomato sauce, heat 1 tablespoon olive oil in a skillet and sauté 2 diced shallots and 2 crushed garlic cloves for 1–2 minutes. Add 1 (14½ oz) can diced tomatoes, a pinch of dried red pepper flakes, 2 teaspoons thyme, and 2 tablespoons white wine. Simmer for 5–6 minutes. Meanwhile, cook 2 (1 lb) packages store-bought gnocchi for 2 minutes in a saucepan of boiling water. Drain and toss the cooked gnocchi in the tomato sauce and serve sprinkled with Parmesan cheese shavings. **Total cooking time 10 minutes.**

coconut dahl with toasted naan

Serves **4**
Total cooking time **10 minutes**

1 tablespoon **vegetable oil**
1 **onion**, coarsely chopped
2 tablespoons **korma curry paste**
²⁄₃ cup **dried red lentils**, rinsed
1 cup **water**
1¾ cups **coconut milk**
black pepper
chopped **fresh cilantro**
naans

Heat the oil in a heavy saucepan and cook the onion over high heat, stirring, for 1 minute, then stir in the curry paste and lentils.

Pour in the coconut milk, then add the measured water. Simmer briskly, uncovered, for 8–9 minutes, until the lentils are tender and the mixture is thick and pulpy. Season with black pepper and sprinkle with the chopped cilantro.

Meanwhile, lightly toast the naans under a preheated high broiler until warm and golden. Cut into strips and serve alongside the dahl for dipping.

For chunky vegetable dahl with toasted naan strips, heat ¼ cup vegetable oil in a large saucepan and cook 1 coarsely chopped onion, 1 trimmed and coarsely chopped large zucchini, and 1 trimmed and coarsely chopped eggplant over medium-high heat, stirring occasionally, for 10 minutes, until tender. Stir in ¼ cup korma curry paste and ²⁄₃ cup rinsed dried red lentils, then pour in 2½ cups vegetable broth and simmer for 10–15 minutes, until thick and pulpy. Meanwhile, prepare the toasted naan strips as above and serve with the dahl. **Total cooking time 30 minutes.**

zucchini & feta fritters

Serves **4**

Total cooking time **20 minutes**

1 **egg**, lightly beaten

3 tablespoons **all-purpose flour**

¼ teaspoon **baking powder**

2 tablespoons **buttermilk**

2 large **zucchini**, grated

handful of **dill**, chopped

3 **scallions**, chopped

5 oz **feta cheese**

⅓ cup **olive oil**

toasted **pita breads**, to serve

Roasted pepper salad

2 **roasted red peppers** from a jar, chopped

1 tablespoon **lemon juice**

2 tablespoons **olive oil**

handful of **mint**, chopped

Mix together the egg, flour, baking powder, and buttermilk until smooth. Place the zucchini in a clean dish towel and squeeze to remove excess water, then mix into the batter along with the dill and scallions. Crumble in the feta.

Heat half the oil in a large nonstick skillet. Add heaping tablespoons of the batter to the pan and press down a little on each fritter with the back of the spoon to flatten slightly. Cook for 3 minutes, until golden brown, then turn and cook for an additional 2 minutes, until golden and cooked through. Drain on paper towels and keep warm. Repeat with the remaining mixture and oil.

Stir together the roasted peppers, lemon juice, oil, and mint. Serve alongside the fritters with some toasted pita breads.

For tangy couscous, zucchini & feta salad, slice 2 zucchini into long, thin strips. Rub with 2 tablespoons olive oil and cook on a hot ridged grill pan for 1 minute on each side until lightly charred. Place 1 ½ cups couscous in a bowl and pour 1¾ cups hot vegetable broth over the grains. Cover and let stand for 5 minutes, then stir in ¼ cup lemon juice, ⅓ cup olive oil, and a handful each of chopped parsley and mint. Season and add ½ cup drained and chopped sun-dried tomatoes in oil and the zucchini. Sprinkle with ⅓ cup toasted pine nuts and ⅔ cup crumbled feta cheese. **Total cooking time 10 minutes.**

tomato risotto

Serves **4**

Total cooking time **30 minutes**

1 tablespoon **olive oil**

1 **onion**, diced

2 **garlic cloves**, crushed

2 **plum tomatoes**

1 cup **tomato sauce**

1¼ cups **hot vegetable broth**

1 cup **risotto rice**

1 cup drained **sun-dried tomatoes in oil** (cut into strips)

2 tablespoons shredded **basil**

salt and **black pepper**

½ cup grated **Parmesan cheese**, to serve

Heat the olive oil in a saucepan and sauté the onion and garlic for 5–6 minutes.

Meanwhile, put the tomatoes into a large bowl and pour boiling water over them. Let stand for 30 seconds, then drain and refresh under cold water. Peel off the skins, then seed and chop the tomatoes.

Put the tomato sauce and broth into a small saucepan and bring to a simmer.

Stir the rice into the onions and continue to stir, for 1–2 minutes, until the edges of the grains look translucent.

Add a ladle of the tomato sauce and broth and stir continuously, until it has all been absorbed. Repeat with the remaining hot broth, adding a ladle at a time, until the rice is "al dente."

Stir in the chopped tomatoes, sliced sun-dried tomatoes, and basil and season.

Serve sprinkled with grated Parmesan.

For quick tomato & rice salad, skin and chop 4 plum tomatoes, as above, and mix with 4 sliced scallions, 2 cups cooked rice, 7 oz mozzarella cheese, diced, and 2 tablespoons chopped basil. Season and sprinkle with 2 tablespoons olive oil to serve. **Total cooking time 10 minutes.**

cheese & spinach calzones

Serves **4**

Total cooking time **30 minutes**

3⅔ cups **white bread flour**,
  plus extra for dusting
2¼ teaspoons **active dry
  yeast**
a pinch of **salt**
3 tablespoons **olive oil**
1¼ cups **warm water**
1 bunch (10 oz) **spinach**
1½ cups **ricotta cheese**
¼ cup grated **Parmesan
  cheese**
¼ cup grated **Pecorino
  cheese**
4 **scallions**, sliced
1 teaspoon **black pepper**

To make the dough, put the flour, yeast, and salt into a large bowl and mix together. Make a well in the center. Stir in 1 tablespoon of the olive oil and most of the measured water. Mix together with your hand, gradually adding more water, if necessary, until you have a soft, but not sticky dough.

Turn the dough out onto a floured work surface and knead for 5–10 minutes, until the dough is smooth and elastic. Divide into 4 pieces and roll each out to 8 inch circles.

Heat the remaining olive oil in a skillet, add the spinach, and cook for 2–3 minutes. Squeeze out the water, transfer to a bowl, and stir in the remaining ingredients.

Divide the mixture among the 4 circles of dough, placing the mixture on one half of each circle, leaving a 1 inch clean edge. Brush the clean edges with water, then fold the other half over the filling and pinch the edges together to seal. Place the calzones on a baking sheet and bake in a preheated oven, at 425°F, for 6–8 minutes, until the dough is cooked and the filling is hot.

For cheese & spinach stuffed pita breads, heat 1 tablespoon olive oil in a skillet and sauté 1 sliced red onion for a few minutes, then add 1 bunch (10 oz) spinach and stir to wilt. Remove from the heat, drain out any water, and mix with ¼ cup grated Parmesan cheese and 7 oz torn mozzarella. Heat 4 pita breads, slice along one side, and open up. Fill each pita with the spinach filling. **Total cooking time 10 minutes.**

feta, scallion & walnut mini tarts

Serves **4**

Total cooking time **10 minutes**

4 slices of **whole wheat bread**, crusts removed

1 cup crumbled **feta cheese**

2 **scallions**, thinly sliced

¼ cup **walnut pieces**, lightly crushed

8 **cherry tomatoes**, cut into quarters

1 tablespoon **olive oil**

salt and **black pepper**

To serve

8 cups **mixed salad greens**

½ **cucumber**, sliced

Roll the bread out thinly using a rolling pin. Cut each slice into a circle, about 5 inches in diameter and press the circles into 4 cups in a large, nonstick muffin pan. Cook in a preheated oven, at 400°F, for 7–8 minutes, until crisp and golden.

Meanwhile, mix the crumbled feta with the scallions, walnut pieces, and tomatoes. Season, then spoon the mixture into the toasted tart shells. Drizzle with the olive oil and serve with a mixed leaf and cucumber salad.

For feta, scallion & walnut tart, Roll 1 sheet ready-to-bake puff pastry into a rectangle measuring about 12 x 8 inches. Place on a lightly greased baking sheet and score a border about ¾ inch in from the edges all the way around the pastry, not quite cutting through. Sprinkle 1½ cups crumbled feta, 4 thinly sliced scallions, ½ cup walnut pieces, and 12 quartered cherry tomatoes over the pastry, keeping within the border. Drizzle with 1 tablespoon olive oil and cook in a preheated oven, at 400°F, for about 20 minutes, until crisp and golden. Serve with salad. **Total cooking time 30 minutes.**

108

delicatessan pasta

Serves **4**
Total cooking time **20 minutes**

12 oz **fusilli**
2 tablespoons **extra virgin olive oil**
1 tablespoon **balsamic vinegar**
½ teaspoon **Dijon mustard**
½ teaspoon **honey**
1 **garlic clove**, crushed
10 **sun-dried tomatoes**, sliced
1 (14 oz) **can artichoke hearts**, drained and halved
4 oz **Parmesan cheese** shavings

Cook the fusilli in a saucepan of boiling water for 9–12 minutes, or according to the package directions.

Whisk together the oil, vinegar, mustard, honey, and garlic to make the dressing.

Drain the pasta and return to the pan with the dressing. Stir in the sun-dried tomatoes and artichoke hearts and stir to warm through.

Serve in shallow pasta bowls, sprinkled with the Parmesan shavings.

For artichoke & sun-dried tomato bruschetta,

slice 2 baguettes into 16 slices and place on a baking sheet. Drizzle with 2 tablespoons olive oil and toast for 2–3 minutes on each side. Rub one side of each slice with a peeled garlic clove. Top the bruschetta with a 1 (14 oz) can artichoke hearts, drained and sliced, and 12 chopped sun-dried tomatoes. Serve sprinkled with 2 tablespoons toasted pine nuts and small basil leaves. **Total cooking time 10 minutes.**

moroccan vegetable stew

Serves **4**

Total cooking time **30 minutes**

1 cup **couscous**

2 cups **boiling water**

2 tablespoons **sunflower oil**

1 large **onion**, finely chopped

2 **garlic cloves**, minced

1 teaspoon grated **fresh ginger root**

2 teaspoons **ground cumin**

1 teaspoon **ground coriander**

2 teaspoons **ground cinnamon**

1 teaspoon **ground turmeric**

2 teaspoons **dried red pepper flakes**

1 tablespoon **harissa paste**

1 (14½ oz) **can diced tomatoes**

1 cup **hot vegetable broth**

2 **red bell peppers**, cored, seeded, and cut into bite-size pieces

1 **small butternut squash** (about 1½ lb), peeled, seeded, and cubed

⅔ cup **golden raisins**

salt and **black pepper**

chopped **fresh cilantro**, to garnish

Put the couscous into a large heatproof bowl and season with salt. Pour the measured water over the grains, cover with plastic wrap, and let stand for 10 minutes, or according to the package directions, until the water is absorbed. Gently fork to separate the grains, then set aside and keep warm.

Meanwhile, heat the oil in a large skillet, add the onion, and cook over medium heat, stirring occasionally, for 2–3 minutes, until softened. Add the garlic, ginger, ground spices, red pepper flakes, harissa, tomatoes, and broth and bring to a boil, then reduce the heat to low, cover, and simmer gently for 10–12 minutes.

Stir in the red bell peppers, squash, and golden raisins, replace the lid, and increase the heat to medium. Simmer for 10–15 minutes or until the vegetables are tender, then season.

Spoon the couscous into warm bowls, then ladle the stew over it and serve sprinkled with chopped cilantro.

For Moroccan kebabs, cut 2 large zucchini, 2 cored and seeded red bell peppers, and 1 eggplant into chunks and put into a large bowl. Mix together ½ cup olive oil, 1 tablespoon harissa paste, the juice of 2 lemons, and a small handful of chopped cilantro, pour the dressing over the vegetables, and toss. Thread the vegetables onto 12 metal skewers, season, and cook under a preheated medium broiler for 10–12 minutes, turning once. Serve with couscous. **Total cooking time 20 minutes.**

quick roasted pepper pizza

Serves **4**
Total cooking time **10 minutes**

4 **pita breads**
¼ cup **ketchup**
4 **roasted red and yellow peppers** from a jar, drained and sliced
4 **scallions**, sliced
4 oz **mozzarella cheese**, sliced
small handful of **arugula**

Toast the pita breads for 2 minutes on each side. Top each one with 1 tablespoon ketchup and the roasted peppers, scallions, and mozzarella.

Place under a preheated hot broiler and cook for 4–6 minutes, until bubbling and golden. Serve topped with the arugula.

For polenta crust roasted pepper pizza, bring 4 cups water to a boil in a large saucepan. Slowly pour in 1¾ cups instant polenta or grits, stirring constantly. Add 1 teaspoon dried oregano, season, and continue to cook, stirring, for 8–10 minutes, or according to the package directions, until the polenta or grits are thick. Divide in half, pour out onto 2 lightly oiled baking sheets, and spread into a circle about ½ inch thick. Bake in a preheated oven, at 400°F, for 12 minutes. Spread 1 (14½ oz) can dice tomatoes over the pizza crust, then top with 2 cups roasted red peppers strips and 10–12 coarsely torn basil leaves and sprinkle with 8 oz sliced mozzarella cheese. Bake for an additional 12–15 minutes, until the cheese is golden and bubbling. Serve hot, cut into wedges. **Total cooking time 40 minutes.**

basil & arugula pesto spaghetti

Serves **4**

Total cooking time **20 minutes**

⅓ cup **sunflower seeds** or **pumpkin seeds**

1 lb **whole wheat spaghetti**

1 **garlic clove**, coarsely chopped

1 small bunch of **basil**

3 cups **arugula**

¼ cup finely grated **Parmesan cheese**, plus extra to serve (optional)

⅓ cup **olive oil**

1 tablespoon **lemon juice**

salt and **black pepper**

Put the seeds into a small, dry skillet and toast gently for 3–4 minutes, shaking the pan frequently, until lightly toasted and golden. Transfer to a plate to cool.

Cook the spaghetti in a large saucepan of lightly salted boiling water for 11–12 minutes, or according to the package directions, until "al dente."

Meanwhile, crush the garlic together with a generous pinch of salt, using a mortar and pestle. Add the basil and arugula, then pound until crushed to a coarse paste.

Add the toasted seeds and pound to a paste, then transfer to a bowl and stir in the cheese, olive oil, and lemon juice. Season with black pepper and more salt, if necessary.

Drain the pasta and toss immediately with the pesto. Divide among 4 shallow bowls and serve with extra cheese, if desired.

For baked creamy gnocchi with pesto, cook 1 (1 lb) package gnocchi in a large saucepan of lightly salted boiling water for about 2 minutes, or according to package directions, until just tender. Meanwhile, mix together ¼ cup store-bought green pesto and 1¼ cups crème fraîche or Greek yogurt. Stir in the cooked gnocchi, then transfer to a large ovenproof dish and sprinkle with 2 tablespoons grated Parmesan cheese. Cook in a preheated oven, at 375°F, for about 20 minutes, until bubbling and golden. Serve with extra arugula, if desired. **Total cooking time 30 minutes.**

polenta fries with a spicy sauce

Serves **2**
Total cooking time **10 minutes**

1 lb **ready-to-heat polenta**
3 tablespoons **all-purpose flour**, for dusting
¼ cup **olive oil**
1½ cups **store-bought spicy tomato sauce**

To serve
arugula
Parmesan cheese shavings

Cut the block of polenta into french fry-shape sticks and dust in the flour, shaking off the excess.

Heat the oil in a skillet and cook the polenta fries over medium-high heat for 2–3 minutes on each side, until crisp and golden. Drain on paper towels and keep warm.

Meanwhile, heat the tomato sauce in a pan. Spoon into small bowls and serve with the polenta fries, arugula, and Parmesan shavings.

For baked spicy polenta, pour 1½ cups spicy tomato sauce into the bottom of a medium ovenproof dish. Layer ½ (18 oz) package ready-to-heat polenta, sliced, over the sauce and top with 2 oz mozzarella, diced, and 2 tablespoons grated Parmesan cheese. Pour another 1 cup spicy tomato sauce over the top and sprinkle with 3 oz mozzarella, diced, and 2 tablespoons grated Parmesan. Bake in a preheated oven, at 425°F, for 20–25 minutes, until golden and bubbling. Serve with a salad, as above. **Total cooking time 30 minutes.**

mediterranean beans

Serves **4**
Total cooking time **10 minutes**

2 tablespoons **extra virgin
    olive oil**
1 **red onion**, diced
1 **garlic clove**, crushed
½ teaspoon **cumin seeds**
1 (15 oz) **can cannellini
    (white kidney) beans**,
    rinsed and drained
6 **cherry tomatoes**, quartered
2 teaspoons chopped **sage**
4 slices of **crusty bread**
salt and **black pepper**
¼ cup grated **Manchego
    cheese**, to serve

Heat the oil in a large skillet, add the onion, and cook
for 1−2 minutes. Add the garlic and cumin seeds and
cook for an additional 2−3 minutes.

Add the beans and mix well to let them soak up the
flavors, then add the tomatoes. Stir in the sage, season
with salt and black pepper, and heat through.

Meanwhile, toast the bread under a preheated hot
broiler for 2−3 minutes on each side. Serve with the
beans on top and a sprinkling of cheese.

For mixed bean goulash, heat 1 tablespoon olive
oil in a large skillet, add 1 large chopped onion and
2 crushed garlic cloves, and gently sauté for 5 minutes,
until softened. Stir in 1½ cups chopped cremini
mushrooms and cook for an additional 3−4 minutes.
Add 1 tablespoon smoked paprika and continue to
cook for 1−2 minutes. Stir in 1 (14½ oz) can diced
tomatoes, 1 cup hot vegetable broth, and 2 cups rinsed
and drained, canned mixed beans, such as kidney
beans, pinto beans, and chickpeas (garbanzo beans).
Bring to a boil, then reduce the heat and simmer for
12−14 minutes, until thick and glossy. Serve with
cooked rice, topped with dollops of sour cream,
if desired. **Total cooking time 30 minutes.**

butternut & broccolini gratin

Serves **4**
Total cooking time **20 minutes**

8 oz **broccolini**, trimmed
½ **butternut squash**, peeled,
    seeded, and chopped
8 oz **mushrooms**, halved
4 tablespoons **butter**
2 tablespoons
   all-purpose flour
1¾ cups **milk**
2 teaspoons **whole-grain**
   mustard
1 cup shredded
   cheddar cheese

Steam the vegetables in a steamer for 8–10 minutes, until tender.

Meanwhile, melt the butter in a small saucepan, then stir in the flour to make a paste. Cook for 1–2 minutes, then gradually whisk in the milk and cook, stirring continuously, until the sauce is thick and smooth. Stir in the mustard and half the shredded cheese.

Transfer the vegetables to an ovenproof dish, pour the sauce over them, and sprinkle with the remaining cheese. Cook under a preheated hot broiler for 5–6 minutes, until bubbling and golden.

For cheesy mashed butternut with broccoli & poached eggs, cook ½ peeled, seeded, and diced butternut squash and 1 peeled and diced russet potato in a saucepan of boiling water for 8 minutes, until tender. Meanwhile, bring a saucepan of water to a gentle simmer and stir with a large spoon to create a swirl. Break 2 eggs into the water and cook for 3 minutes. Remove with a slotted spoon and keep warm. Repeat with another 2 eggs. In a separate pan, steam 1 small bunch broccoli, cut into florets, until tender. Drain the squash and potatoes, then mash in the pan with ¾ cup shredded cheddar cheese. Serve topped with the broccoli and poached eggs, sprinkled with 2 tablespoons grated Parmesan cheese. **Total cooking time 10 minutes.**

tomato & eggplant pappardelle

Serves **4**
Total cooking time **30 minutes**

¼ cup **extra virgin olive oil**
1 large **eggplant**, cut into
  ¾ inch dice
1 small **onion**, finely diced
2 **garlic cloves**, crushed
1½ cups **tomato and
  basil sauce**
12 oz **dried pappardelle**
  or **tagliatelle**
8 oz **mozzarella cheese**,
  diced
black pepper

To garnish (optional)
¼ cup grated **Parmesan
  cheese**
basil, coarsely torn

Heat the oil in a large skillet over medium-high heat. Add the eggplant and onion and cook, stirring, for 5 minutes.

Add the garlic and cook for 1 minute. Add the tomato sauce and 1 cup water to the pan, bring to a simmer, and cook for 8–10 minutes, or until the eggplants are just tender. Season.

Meanwhile, cook the pasta in boiling water according to the package directions. Remove from the heat, drain, and return to the pan.

Stir the mozzarella into the sauce until it begins to melt slightly, then add to the pasta. Toss to mix well and season with black pepper. Garnish with the grated Parmesan and basil, if desired.

For tomato, eggplant & mozzarella pizzas, place 2 store-bought pizza crusts on 2 baking sheets and spread with the tomato and eggplant sauce from the above recipe. Sprinkle with 8 oz mozzarella cheese, diced, and cook in a preheated oven, at 425°F, for 8–10 minutes. Serve immediately. **Total cooking time 10 minutes.**

fava bean & feta tagliatelle

Serves **4**
Total cooking time **10 minutes**

12 oz **tagliatelle**
2 cups **fresh** or **frozen**
   fava beans
2 tablespoons **olive oil**
6 **scallions**, sliced
½ teaspoon **dried red**
   pepper flakes
3 cups coarsely chopped
   watercress or **other**
   peppery greens
grated zest of **1 lemon**
1⅓ cups crumbled
   feta cheese
2 tablespoons **toasted**
   pine nuts

Cook the pasta in a large saucepan of boiling water for 8–9 minutes, or according to the package directions, until "al dente." Add the fava beans 3 minutes before the end of the cooking time.

Meanwhile, heat the oil in a large skillet, add the scallions and red pepper flakes, and cook for 2–3 minutes. Stir in the watercress and lemon zest.

Drain the pasta and beans and add to the watercress mixture with the feta. Mix well.

Serve sprinkled with the toasted pine nuts.

For fava bean & feta salad, put 1½ cups couscous into a large heatproof bowl and just cover with boiling water. Let stand for 10–12 minutes. Meanwhile, cook 2 cups frozen fava beans in a saucepan of boiling water for 4–5 minutes, until tender, then drain. Heat 1 tablespoon olive oil in a skillet, add 4 cups baby spinach, and cook briefly until wilted. Fluff up the couscous with a fork, then stir in the fava beans, spinach, 2 tablespoons chopped mint, ¾ cup sliced pitted black ripe olives, and 1½ cups crumbled feta cheese. Whisk together the juice of ½ lemon and 2 tablespoons olive oil in a small bowl, then drizzle the dressing over the salad and serve. **Total cooking time 20 minutes.**

mixed mushroom stroganoff

Serves **4**

Total cooking time **20 minutes**

¼ cup **olive oil**

1 **onion**, finely chopped

12 oz **cremini mushrooms**,
   trimmed and quartered

6 oz **shiitake mushrooms**,
   trimmed and halved

4 oz **oyster mushrooms**,
   trimmed and halved

1 tablespoon **brandy**

1 teaspoon **Dijon mustard**

1 cup **crème fraîche** or
   sour cream

black pepper

To serve

cooked brown or **white**
   long-grain rice

¼ cup chopped
   flat leaf parsley

Heat the oil in a large, heavy skillet and cook the onion over medium heat, stirring frequently, for 2–3 minutes, until softened. Add the cremini mushrooms and cook, stirring frequently, for 5 minutes, until lightly browned. Add the shiitake and oyster mushrooms and cook, stirring frequently, for 5 minutes, until softened.

Pour the brandy into the mushroom mixture and stir over high heat until evaporated. Mix the mustard into the crème fraîche or sour cream, then spoon into the pan and heat for 2 minutes, until piping hot. Season well with black pepper.

Serve the stroganoff over cooked brown or white long-grain rice, with the parsley sprinkled over the top.

For mushroom stroganoff on whole-grain toast,
thickly slice 8 oz trimmed cremini mushrooms and 8 oz trimmed portobello mushrooms. Melt 2 tablespoons garlic butter in a large skillet, add the mushrooms, and cook over high heat, stirring frequently, for 4–5 minutes. Meanwhile, toast and butter 4 thick slices of whole-grain bread. Stir 1 tablespoon whole-grain mustard and 1¼ cups sour cream into the mushrooms. Season and serve on the toast with 1 tablespoon chopped chives sprinkled over. **Total cooking time 10 minutes.**

pasta with blue cheese & spinach

Serves **4**
Total cooking time **20 minutes**

1 lb **fettucine**
1 tablespoon **olive oil**
1 **onion**, chopped
2 **garlic cloves**, crushed
1¼ cups **light cream**
4 oz **gorgonzola dolce** or
  other **blue cheese**
1 (6 oz) package **baby
  spinach**
salt and **black pepper**

Cook the fettucine in a saucepan of boiling water according to the package directions, until "al dente."

Meanwhile, heat the olive oil in a skillet and sauté the onion and garlic for 4–5 minutes. Add the cream and simmer for 5–6 minutes, until the cream thickens a little.

Stir in the cheese and spinach and stir for 1 minute. Drain the pasta and add to the spinach. Season with salt and black pepper, then gently mix together and serve in warm bowls.

For blue cheese & spinach soup, heat 1 tablespoon olive oil in a saucepan and sauté 1 chopped onion and 2 chopped garlic cloves for 3–4 minutes. Stir in 1 chopped white round potato and cook for an additional 1–2 minutes. Pour in 2 cups vegetable broth and bring to a boil. Simmer for 10 minutes, then stir in 2½ cups milk and bring to a simmer again. Add 6 cups baby spinach and the grated zest of 1 lemon and cook for 5–6 minutes, then stir in another 6 cups baby spinach and 2 oz gorgonzola dolce or other blue cheese. Using an immersion blender, or in a food processor or blender, blend the soup until smooth. Season and serve the soup with toasted pumpkin seeds and a few more crumbs of blue cheese. **Total cooking time 30 minutes.**

patatas bravas

Serves **4**
Total cooking time **30 minutes**

7 **russet** or **Yukon Gold
  potatoes** (about 1¾ lb),
  peeled and cut into
  small cubes

2 tablespoons **olive oil**

1 (14½ oz) **can diced
  tomatoes**

1 small **red onion,**
  finely chopped

2 **garlic cloves**, finely chopped

1 teaspoon **dried red
  pepper flakes**

1 teaspoon **cayenne pepper**

3 teaspoons **sweet
  smoked paprika**

1 **bay leaf**

1 teaspoon **sugar**

salt and **black pepper**

finely chopped **flat leaf
  parsley,** to garnish

crusty bread, to serve

Cook the potatoes in a large saucepan of salted boiling water for 10–12 minutes or until tender, then drain well.

Line a baking sheet with nonstick parchment paper. Place the potatoes in a single layer on the sheet, drizzle with the oil, and season. Place in a preheated oven, at 425°F, for 10–12 minutes or until lightly browned.

Meanwhile, put the tomatoes, red onion, garlic, red pepper flakes, and cayenne pepper into a saucepan and cook over medium heat for 10 minutes, stirring occasionally, then stir in the paprika, bay leaf, and sugar and cook for an additional 4–5 minutes, until thickened. Remove and discard the bay leaf.

Transfer the potatoes to a warm serving dish, then pour the spicy tomato sauce over them and toss to mix well. Sprinkle with chopped parsley and serve with crusty bread.

For spicy potato & tomato stir-fry, heat 2 tablespoons sunflower oil in a large wok or skillet until hot, add 1 drained (15 oz) can new potatoes, cubed, 1 coarsely chopped onion, 1 teaspoon dried red pepper flakes, 1 tablespoon sweet smoked paprika, and 2 diced plum tomatoes, and stir-fry over high heat for 5–6 minutes or until piping hot, then season. Serve with a green salad and warm bread. **Total cooking time 10 minutes.**

lentil bolognese

1 **onion**, coarsely chopped
1 **carrot**, peeled and chopped
1 **celery stick**, coarsely
  chopped
1 **garlic clove**, peeled
3 tablespoons **olive oil**
½ cup **red wine**
½ cup **water**
¼ cup **tomato paste**
1 (14½ oz) **can diced
  tomatoes**
1 teaspoon **dried mixed
  herbs**
4 cups **cooked green lentils**
salt and **black pepper**

To serve
½ cup grated **Parmesan
  cheese**
crusty bread

Put the onion, carrot, celery, and garlic into a food processor and pulse briefly until finely chopped. Heat the olive oil in a large, heavy casserole or saucepan. Add the vegetable mixture and cook for 5–6 minutes, stirring frequently, until softened and lightly golden.

Pour in the red wine, measured water, tomato paste, diced tomatoes, and herbs, and season with salt and black pepper. Simmer gently for about 15 minutes, then add the lentils and simmer for an additional 5–7 minutes, until thickened and tender. Spoon into deep bowls, sprinkle with cheese and serve with plenty of fresh, crusty bread.

For quick lentil Bolognese, put 1 coarsely chopped onion, 1 peeled and coarsely chopped carrot, 1 coarsely chopped celery stick, and 1 garlic clove into a food processor and pulse until finely chopped. Heat 3 tablespoons olive oil in a large, heavy casserole or saucepan and cook the vegetable mixture for 5–6 minutes, stirring frequently, until softened and lightly golden. Stir in 2 cups prepared tomato sauce and 4 cups cooked green lentils. Simmer gently for 2–3 minutes, then serve as above, with grated Parmesan cheese and crusty bread. **Total cooking time 10 minutes.**

hot & spicy

spicy eggplant & tomato curry

Serves **4**
Total cooking time **30 minutes**

2 large **eggplants**
½ cup **vegetable oil**
2 **onions**, thinly sliced
6 **garlic cloves**, finely chopped
1 tablespoon peeled and
    grated finely chopped **fresh
    ginger root**
2 **red chiles**, seeded and
    thinly sliced
¾ cup **canned diced
    tomatoes**
6 **kaffir lime leaves**
1 tablespoon **ketjap manis
    (thick soy sauce)**
2 tablespoons **dark soy sauce**
1 teaspoon packed **light
    brown sugar**
juice of **1 lime**
small handful of chopped
    fresh cilantro leaves
2 tablespoons chopped
    roasted peanuts
steamed noodles or **rice**,
    to serve

Cut the eggplants into finger-thick batons. Reserve 1 tablespoon of the oil, then heat the remaining oil in a large skillet, add the eggplants, and sauté over medium heat, stirring occasionally, for 5–6 minutes or until lightly browned. Remove with a slotted spoon and drain on paper towels.

Heat the reserved oil in the skillet, add the onions and garlic, and sauté over medium heat, stirring occasionally, for 6–7 minutes, until softened and lightly browned. Add the ginger, red chiles, tomatoes, and lime leaves and cook for 2–3 minutes, stirring frequently. Return the eggplants to the pan with a splash of water and simmer gently for 2–3 minutes.

Remove from the heat and stir in the kecap manis, soy sauce, sugar, lime juice, and chopped cilantro.

Spoon into warm bowls, sprinkle with the chopped peanuts and serve with steamed noodles or rice.

For spicy eggplant & tomato salad, drain
1 (12–14 oz) jar or can of chargrilled eggplants in olive oil, reserving the oil, and put the eggplants into a salad bowl with 8 sliced plum tomatoes and a handful of arugula. Mix ⅓ cup of the reserved oil, the juice of 2 lemons, and 1 teaspoon chili paste in a bowl, then season. Pour the dressing over the salad, toss to mix well, and serve with crusty bread. **Total cooking time 10 minutes.**

tofu with bok choy & scallions

Serves **4**
Total cooking time **20 minutes**

2 tablespoons **sunflower oil**
2 teaspoons grated **fresh ginger root**
8 **garlic cloves**, coarsely chopped
4 **shallots**, finely chopped
2 **red chiles**, seeded and chopped
3 inch length of **trimmed lemon grass stalk**, finely chopped
1 teaspoon **ground turmeric**
1¾ cups **coconut milk**
1 cup **hot vegetable broth**
12 oz **baby bok choy**, halved or quartered
3 cups **snow peas**
1 (16 oz) package **firm tofu**, drained and cubed
1 tablespoon **dark soy sauce**
1 tablespoon **lime juice**
6 **scallions**, thinly sliced
salt and **black pepper**

To garnish
small handful of **Thai basil**
sliced **red chiles**

Put the oil, ginger, garlic, shallots, red chiles, lemon grass, turmeric, and half the coconut milk into a food processor or blender and blend until fairly smooth.

Heat a large, nonstick wok or skillet until hot, add the coconut milk mixture, and stir-fry over high heat for 3–4 minutes. Add the remaining coconut milk and the broth and bring to a boil, then reduce the heat to low and simmer gently, uncovered, for 6–8 minutes.

Add the bok choy, snow peas, and tofu and simmer for an additional 6–7 minutes. Stir in the soy sauce and lime juice, then season and simmer for another 1–2 minutes.

Remove from the heat and stir in the scallions. Ladle into warm bowls and serve sprinkled with Thai basil and sliced red chiles.

For Japanese-style tofu with scallions, drain 2 (16 oz) packages firm tofu, cut into cubes, and put into a dish. Mix together 1 tablespoon sesame oil, 2 tablespoons sunflower oil, 1 tablespoon mirin, ¼ cup light soy sauce, 1 seeded and diced red chile, and 1 teaspoon chili powder mixed with 1 teaspoon sesame seeds and drizzle over the tofu. Sprinkle with 8 thinly sliced scallions and serve. **Total cooking time 10 minutes.**

spicy zucchini penne

Serves **4**
Total cooking time **20 minutes**

1 tablespoon **butter**
1 tablespoon **olive oil**
2 **red chiles**, finely chopped
2 **garlic cloves**, finely chopped
4 **scallions**, very finely
   chopped
3 **zucchini**, coarsely grated
finely grated zest of **1 lime**
²⁄₃ cup **cream cheese**
12 oz **dried pennette** or
   other **short-shape pasta**
small handful of **flat leaf
   parsley**, chopped
salt and **black pepper**

Heat the butter and oil in a large skillet, add the red chiles, garlic, scallions, and zucchini, and cook over medium-low heat for 10 minutes or until softened.

Reduce the heat to low, add the lime zest, and gently cook for 3–4 minutes, then add the cream cheese and mix together until the cheese melts. Season.

Meanwhile, cook the pasta in a large saucepan of lightly salted boiling water according to the package directions until "al dente."

Drain the pasta and stir into the zucchini mixture with the parsley. Spoon into warm bowls and serve.

For spicy zucchini stir-fry noodles, heat
2 tablespoons olive oil in a large skillet, add
6 sliced scallions, 2 crushed garlic cloves,
1 chopped red chile, and 2 shredded zucchini,
and cook over high heat for 4–5 minutes, until
softened, then add 1¼ lb fresh egg noodles and
¼ cup light soy sauce and toss to mix well. Stir-fry
for 1–2 minutes or until piping hot. Serve immediately.
Total cooking time 10 minutes.

thai massaman squash curry

Serves **4**

Total cooking time **20 minutes**

2 tablespoons **vegetable oil**

2 tablespoons **Thai massaman curry paste**

6 **shallots**, thinly sliced

3 inch length of **trimmed lemon grass stalk**, finely chopped

6 **green cardamom pods**

2 teaspoons **black mustard seeds**

1 **butternut squash** or **acorn squash** (about 1¾ lb), peeled, seeded, and cut into ½ inch cubes

1 cup **hot vegetable broth**

1¾ cups **coconut milk**

juice of **1 lime**

To garnish

small handful of **Thai basil** or **mint**

thin red chile slices

To serve (optional)

lime wedges

steamed jasmine rice

Heat the oil in a heavy saucepan, add the curry paste, shallots, lemon grass, cardamom, and mustard seeds, and sauté over medium heat for 1–2 minutes, until fragrant.

Add the squash and pour in the broth and coconut milk. Bring to a simmer, then cook for 10–12 minutes or until the squash is tender.

Remove from the heat and stir in the lime juice. Ladle into warm bowls, then sprinkle with Thai basil or mint along with red chile slices. Serve with lime wedges for squeezing over the curry and with steamed jasmine rice, if desired.

For spicy roast Thai massaman vegetables, peel, seed, and dice ½ butternut squash or acorn squash (about 1 lb) into ¾ inch cubes, core, seed, and dice 2 red bell peppers into ¾ inch cubes, and dice 1 large eggplant into ¾ inch cubes. Put the diced vegetables into an ovenproof dish. Mix together 2 tablespoons Thai massaman curry paste and 1 cup coconut milk in a bowl. Pour the mixture over the vegetables, toss to mix well, and season with salt. Put into a preheated oven, at 400°F, for 20–25 minutes or until tender. Sprinkle with a small handful of Thai basil or mint and serve with steamed rice. **Total cooking time 30 minutes.**

cumin potatoes with pomegranate

Serves **4**
Total cooking time **10 minutes**

½ large **pomegranate**
¼ cup **sunflower oil**
1–2 teaspoons **black mustard
  seeds**
1 teaspoon **hot chili powder**
4 teaspoons **cumin seeds**
2 teaspoons **sesame seeds**
8–10 fresh **curry leaves**
  (optional)
2 teaspoons **ground cumin**
2 teaspoons **ground
  coriander**
1 teaspoon **ground turmeric**
4 **cooked Yukon Gold** or
  russet potatoes, cut into
  1 inch cubes
⅓ cup chopped **fresh
  cilantro leaves**
juice of 1 small **lemon**
salt and **black pepper**

To remove the pomegranate seeds, place the pomegranate over a bowl, cut side down, and hit with the back of a spoon, catching the seeds in the bowl. Set aside.

Heat the oil in a large wok or skillet until hot, add the mustard seeds, and cook over medium-high heat for a few minute, until the seeds begin to pop. Add the chili powder, cumin seeds, sesame seeds, and curry leaves, if using, and stir-fry for 30 seconds, until fragrant.

Add the ground spices and potatoes, season well, then increase the heat to high and stir-fry briskly for 4–5 minutes.

Remove from the heat and stir in the chopped cilantro and pomegranate seeds. Stir in the lemon juice, then spoon into a warm serving dish and serve hot.

For roast cumin potato wedges, cut 9 large baking potatoes (about 2¼ lb) into wedges and cook in a saucepan of boiling water for 6–8 minutes. Drain well, then put into a large bowl. Mix together 1 tablespoon cumin seeds, 1 teaspoon black mustard seeds, 2 teaspoons crushed coriander seeds, 1 tablespoon hot curry powder, and ⅓ cup sunflower oil, season with salt, then drizzle the mixture over the potatoes. Toss to mix well. Spread the potatoes in a single layer on a nonstick baking sheet and put into a preheated oven, at 425°F, for 20–25 minutes. **Total cooking time 30 minutes.**

green lentil & lima bean salad

Serves **4**
Total cooking time **10 minutes**

2 cups **cooked green lentils**
1 (15 oz) **can lima beans**,
   rinsed and drained
1 **red onion**, finely sliced
12 **cherry tomatoes**, halved
1 cup coarsely chopped
   flat leaf parsley

Dressing
⅓ cup **extra-virgin olive oil**
2 **red chiles**, finely diced
2 tablespoons **red wine
   vinegar**
1 teaspoon **Dijon** or **whole-
   grain mustard**
1 teaspoon **honey**
½ **garlic clove**, crushed

Put the lentils and lima beans into a large serving bowl, then add the onion, cherry tomatoes, and parsley.

Mix together all the dressing ingredients in a small bowl, then pour it over the salad, toss to mix well, and serve.

For spicy green lentil & lima bean pasta, cook 12 oz orzo pasta in a large saucepan of lightly salted boiling water according to the package directions until just "al dente," then drain and return to the pan. Cover and keep warm. Heat 2 tablespoons sunflower oil in a large skillet, add 1 sliced red onion, 2 sliced red chiles, and 2 sliced garlic cloves, and cook over medium heat, stirring occasionally, for 5–6 minutes, until softened. Stir in 2 cups cooked green lentils, 1 (15 oz) can lima beans, rinsed and drained, ¾ cup hot vegetable broth, and the cooked orzo and bring to a boil, then reduce the heat to medium, cover, and cook for 5–6 minutes, stirring occasionally. Season, then stir in a small handful of chopped flat leaf parsley and serve. **Total cooking time 30 minutes.**

vegetable tempura with chili sauce

Serves **4**
Total cooking time **20 minutes**

vegetable oil, for deep-frying
1 large **red bell pepper**,
   cored, seeded, and cut
   into chunks
10 **baby corn**
2 cups **broccoli florets**
4 oz **asparagus spears**,
   trimmed
6 large **scallions**, cut into
   2 inch lengths
sweet chili dipping sauce,
   to serve

Batter
3 tablespoons **all-purpose
   flour**
⅓ cup plus **1** tablespoon
   cornstarch
2 **eggs**, beaten
⅓ cup **beer**
salt

Make the batter. Sift the flour and cornstarch into a bowl and season with a little salt. Make a well in the center, add the eggs, and whisk a little, then gradually add the beer, pouring it in slowly and whisking continuously to make a smooth batter.

Fill a deep saucepan halfway with vegetable oil and heat to 375°F, or until a cube of bread browns in 30 seconds. Working quickly, dip the vegetable pieces, one by one, into the batter. Deep-fry, in batches, in the hot oil for 1–2 minutes, until lightly golden.

Remove with a slotted spoon, drain on paper towels, and keep warm. Serve with sweet chili dipping sauce.

For sweet chili & tempura vegetable noodles, cook the Vegetable Tempura as above. Meanwhile, cook 8 oz soba noodles in a saucepan of lightly salted boiling water according to the package directions, until "al dente," adding 1½ cups trimmed green beans for the final 5 minutes of cooking time. Drain well. In a large wok, toss the tempura with the noodles and beans. Mix together ½ cup sweet chili sauce, 3 tablespoons soy sauce, and 3 tablespoons sesame oil in a small bowl, then toss into the noodles. Serve hot. **Total cooking time 30 minutes.**

spinach, tomato & paneer curry

Serves **4**
Total cooking time **30 minutes**

1½ bunches **spinach**
  (about 1 lb)
3 tablespoons **butter**
2 teaspoons **cumin seeds**
1 **red chile,** seeded and finely
  chopped
1 **onion,** finely chopped
2 **plum tomatoes,** finely
  chopped
2 teaspoons minced **garlic**
1 tablespoon peeled and finely
  grated **fresh ginger root**
1 teaspoon **chili powder**
1 teaspoon **ground coriander**
8 oz paneer **(Indian cottage
  cheese)** or firm tofu, cut
  into bite-size pieces
2 tablespoons **heavy cream**
1 teaspoon **lemon juice**
2 tablespoons finely chopped
  fresh cilantro leaves
salt and **black pepper**
flatbreads, to serve (optional)

Cook the spinach in a large saucepan of boiling water
for 2–3 minutes, then drain well. Transfer to a food
processor or blender and process to a smooth puree.

Heat the butter in a large wok or skillet, add the cumin
seeds, red chile, and onion, and stir-fry over medium-low
heat for 6–8 minutes, until the onions have softened.
Add the tomatoes, garlic, ginger, chili powder, and
ground coriander and season well. Stir through and
cook for 2–3 minutes.

Increase the heat to high, add the paneer or tofu, and
stir-fry for 1–2 minutes, then add the spinach puree
and stir-fry for an additional 4–5 minutes, until well
mixed and heated through.

Remove from the heat and stir in the cream, lemon
juice, and chopped cilantro. Spoon into warm bowls
and serve with warm flatbreads, if desired.

For spicy spinach, tomato & cottage cheese salad,
put 3 cups baby spinach and 3 cups halved cherry
tomatoes into a salad bowl. Mix together 1½ cups
cottage cheese, 1 teaspoon ginger paste, 1 teaspoon
garlic paste, 1 teaspoon chili paste, and 2 teaspoons
toasted cumin seeds in a bowl, then season. Add to
the spinach and tomatoes, toss gently to mix, and serve
with crusty bread or warm baguettes. **Total cooking
time 10 minutes.**

spiced okra, tomato & coconut

Serves **4**
Total cooking time **20 minutes**

2 tablespoons **sunflower oil**
6–8 fresh **curry leaves**
2 teaspoons **black mustard seeds**
1 **onion**, finely chopped
2 teaspoons **ground cumin**
1 teaspoon **ground coriander**
2 teaspoons **medium** or **hot curry powder**
1 teaspoon **ground turmeric**
3 **garlic cloves**, finely chopped
1 lb **okra**, trimmed and cut diagonally into 1 inch pieces
2 **ripe plum tomatoes**, chopped
3 tablespoons grated **fresh coconut**, to garnish
salt and **black pepper**

Heat the oil in a large wok or skillet until hot, add the curry leaves, mustard seeds, and onion and stir-fry over medium heat for 3–4 minutes, until fragrant and the onion is beginning to soften. Add the cumin, ground coriander, curry powder, and turmeric and stir-fry for an additional 30 seconds, until fragrant.

Add the garlic and okra, increase the heat to high, and stir-fry for 2–3 minutes, then add the tomatoes and season well. Cover, then reduce the heat to low and cook gently, stirring occasionally, for 10–12 minutes or until the okra is just tender.

Remove from the heat and sprinkle with the coconut, then ladle into warm bowls and serve.

For tomato, coconut & okra curry, heat 2 tablespoons sunflower oil in a large saucepan, add 1 chopped onion, and cook over medium heat, stirring occasionally, for 4–5 minutes, until softened. Stir in 1 (14½ oz) can diced tomatoes and 2 tablespoons medium or hot curry powder, increase the heat to high, and cook for 4–5 minutes, then add 1¾ cups coconut milk and bring back to a boil. Add 1 lb okra, trimmed and cut into ¾ inch pieces, then reduce the heat to medium, cover, and simmer gently for 10–12 minutes or until the okra is just tender. Season well. Serve with steamed rice and warm naans or other flatbreads. **Total cooking time 30 minutes.**

spicy tabbouleh with roasted veg

Serves **4**

Total cooking time **30 minutes**

1 **zucchini**, cut into bite-size pieces

2 **red bell peppers**, cored, seeded, and cut into bite-size pieces

1 **yellow bell pepper**, cored, seeded, and cut into bite-size pieces

¼ cup **olive oil**

3 **garlic cloves**, crushed

1 **red chile,** finely chopped

2 tablespoons **harissa paste**

1 cup **bulgur**

2½ cups **hot vegetable broth**

juice of **1 lemon**

⅓ cup finely chopped **fresh cilantro leaves**

⅓ cup finely chopped **mint**

Put the zucchini and bell peppers into a roasting pan. Mix together the oil, garlic, red chile, and harissa in a bowl, then pour over the vegetables and toss to coat evenly. Place in a preheated oven, at 400°F, for 20 minutes or until softened and the vegetables are just beginning to char at the edges.

Meanwhile, put the bulgur in a large heatproof bowl and pour the broth over the grains, then cover tightly with plastic wrap and let stand for 15 minutes, until the grains are tender but still have a little bite.

Let the bulgur cool slightly, then add the roasted vegetables, lemon juice, and chopped herbs and toss to mix well. Serve warm or at room temperature.

For Moroccan vegetable couscous salad,

put 1 (1 lb) store-bought, fresh Moroccan-style couscous salad into a large bowl with 2½ cups mixed salad greens, 2 (7 oz) jars chargrilled peppers in olive oil, drained, and a small handful each of chopped cilantro leaves and mint. Season, then toss to mix well and serve. **Total cooking time 10 minutes.**

thai vegetable curry

Serves **4**
Total cooking time **20 minutes**

½ **butternut squash** or **acorn
squash** (about 1 lb), peeled,
seeded, and cut into chunks
2 **red bell peppers**, cored,
seeded, and cut into chunks
12 **baby corn**, halved
2 cups **cauliflower florets**
2 tablespoons **Thai green
curry paste**
3½ cups **coconut milk**
⅔ cup **vegetable broth**
3 cups **snow peas**
2 tablespoons **cold water**
1 tablespoon **cornstarch**
¼ cup chopped **fresh cilantro**
Thai jasmine rice, to serve
(optional)

Put the squash, red bell peppers, corn, and cauliflower
into a large, heavy saucepan, add the curry paste,
coconut milk, and broth, and bring to a boil. Reduce the
heat, cover with a lid, and simmer for 15 minutes, until
the vegetables are tender, adding the snow peas for
the final 5 minutes of cooking.

Blend the measured water with the cornstarch, add to
the curry, and cook, stirring constantly, until it thickens
slightly. Stir in the cilantro and serve with Thai Jasmine
rice, if desired.

For Thai corn & cauliflower curried soup, put
2 cups chopped cauliflower florets into a large, heavy
saucepan with 3½ cups coconut milk, 2 tablespoons
Thai green curry paste, ⅔ cup vegetable broth, and
12 halved baby corn. Cook, stirring occasionally, for
9 minutes over high heat. Stir in ¼ cups chopped
fresh cilantro before serving. **Total cooking time
10 minutes.**

spicy kidney beans with rice

Serves **4**
Total cooking time **20 minutes**

1½ cups **long-grain rice**
2 tablespoons **olive** or
    vegetable oil
1 large **red onion**, chopped
1 **red bell pepper**, cored,
    seeded, and chopped
2 **celery sticks**, chopped
2 teaspoons **Cajun-** or
    Mexican-style spice blend
2 (15 oz) **cans red kidney
    beans**, drained and rinsed
3 **ripe tomatoes**, diced
1 tablespoon **red wine
    vinegar**
1 teaspoon **Tabasco sauce,**
    plus extra to serve
½ cup **water**
salt and **black pepper**
2 tablespoons **chopped
    chives**, to garnish (optional)
¼ cup **crème fraîche** or **sour
    cream**, to serve (optional)

Bring a large saucepan of lightly salted water to a boil and cook the rice according to package directions, until just tender. Drain and keep hot.

Meanwhile, heat the oil in a large, deep skillet and add the onion, bell pepper, and celery. Cook for 8–9 minutes, until softened. Add the spice mix, cook for 1 minute, then stir in the kidney beans, tomatoes, vinegar, Tabasco, and measured water.

Cover and simmer gently for 7–8 minutes, adding a little more water, if necessary. Season and sprinkle with the chopped chives, if using. Serve with the rice, extra Tabasco, and crème fraîche or sour cream, if desired.

For spicy Mexican rice salad, seed and finely chop 1 red bell pepper and mix with ½ red onion, finely chopped, and 2 finely chopped celery sticks. Stir in 1½ cups cooked wild and long-grain rice and 1 (15 oz) can of kidney beans, rinsed and drained. Add 2 seeded and chopped tomatoes, 2 tablespoons chopped chives, and 2 tablespoons lime juice. Season generously and serve with lightly salted tortilla chips. **Total cooking time 10 minutes.**

marinated tofu with vegetables

Serves **4**
Total cooking time **30 minutes**

3 tablespoons **ketjap manis**
  or **sweet soy sauce**
1 teaspoon crushed **garlic**
2 teaspoons minced **fresh**
  ginger root
2 tablespoons **sweet chili**
  dipping sauce
1 (16 oz) package **firm tofu**,
  cut into ¾ inch slices
2 tablespoons **vegetable oil**
  or **peanut oil**
1 **carrot**, peeled and cut into
  fine matchsticks
1 lb **bok choy**, sliced
2 cups **bean sprouts**
1 (8 oz) **can bamboo shoots**
  in water
⅓ cup **oyster sauce**
2 teaspoons **sesame seeds**,
  to garnish (optional)

Mix the ketjap manis, garlic, ginger, and sweet chili dipping sauce in a small bowl. Arrange the tofu slices in a shallow dish and pour the marinade over them, turning to coat. Let marinate for about 20 minutes.

Transfer the tofu slices to an aluminum foil-lined broiler rack, reserving the marinade. Cook under a preheated hot broiler for about 3 minutes on each side, until golden. Remove from the heat and keep warm.

Meanwhile, heat the oil in a wok over medium heat. Stir-fry the carrot and bok choy for 4–5 minutes, until beginning to soften. Add the bean sprouts and bamboo shoots and cook for 1 minute, then pour in the remaining marinade and the oyster sauce.

Spoon the vegetables into deep bowls, top with the broiled tofu slices, and sprinkle with sesame seeds, if using.

For tofu & vegetable noodles, cook the stir-fried vegetables following the recipe above, adding ⅔ cup prepared marinated tofu strips or cubed firm tofu, along with the bean sprouts and bamboo shoots. Meanwhile, cook 8 oz medium dried egg noodles according to the package directions, then drain and toss with the vegetables and tofu. Serve with soy sauce. **Total cooking time 20 minutes.**

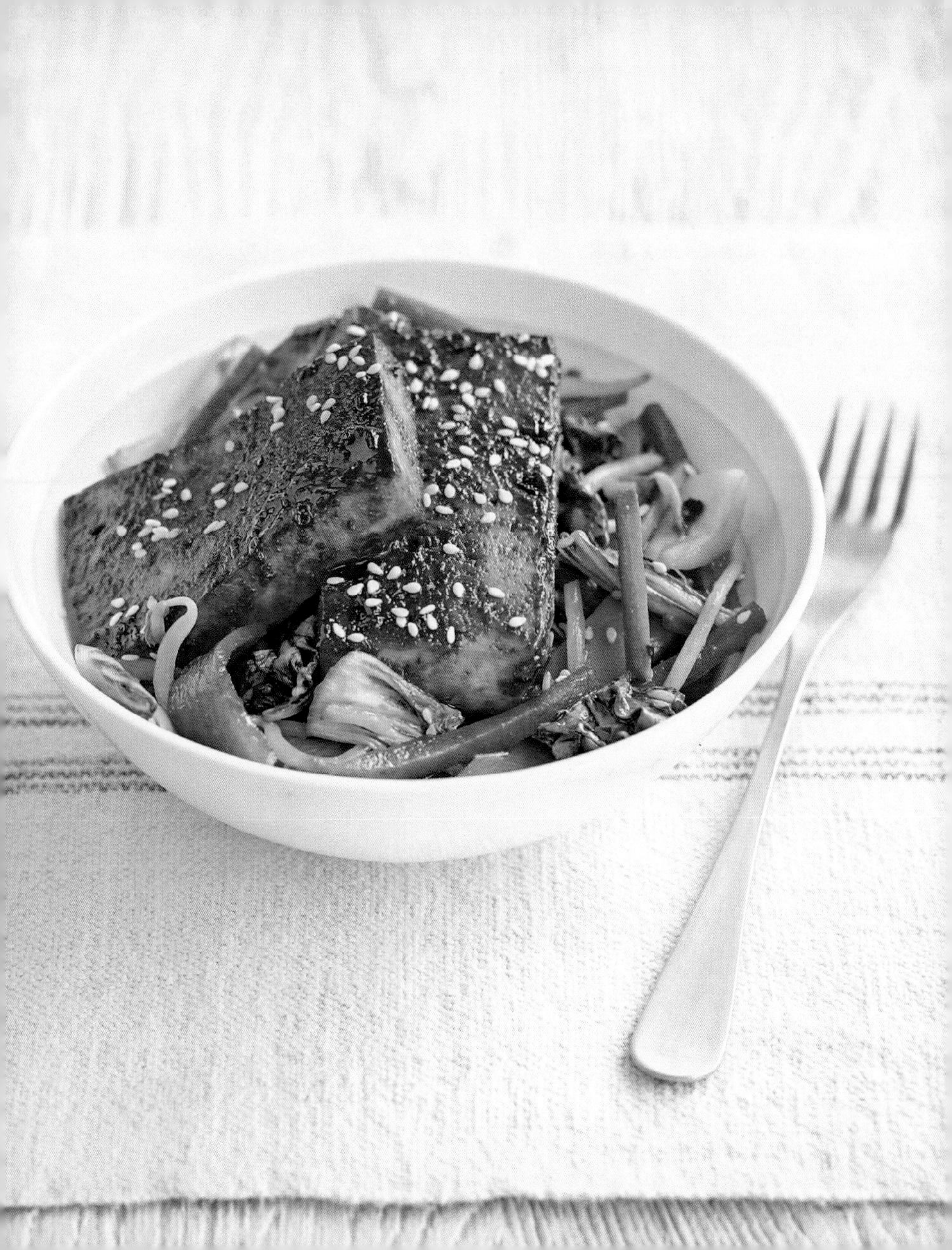

spicy chickpea curry

Serves **4**
Total cooking time **30 minutes**

2 tablespoons **sunflower oil**
4 **garlic cloves**, crushed
2 teaspoons peeled and finely
  grated **fresh ginger root**
1 large **onion**, coarsely grated
1–2 **green chiles**, finely sliced
1 teaspoon **hot chili powder**
1 tablespoon **ground cumin**
1 tablespoon **ground
  coriander**
3 tablespoons **plain yogurt**,
  plus extra, whisked, to serve
2 teaspoons **garam masala**
2 cups **water**
2 teaspoons **tamarind paste**
2 teaspoons **medium** or **hot
  curry powder**
2 (15 oz) **cans chickpeas
  (garbanzo beans)**, rinsed
  and drained
chopped **fresh cilantro
  leaves**, to garnish
lemon wedges, to serve
  (optional)

Heat the oil in a large, heavy skillet, add the garlic, ginger, onion, and green chiles, and cook over medium heat, stirring occasionally, for 5–6 minutes, until the onion is lightly golden. Add the chili powder, cumin, ground coriander, yogurt, and garam masala and cook for an additional 1–2 minutes.

Stir in the measured water and bring to a boil. Add the tamarind paste, curry powder, and chickpeas (garbanzo beans) and bring back to a boil, then reduce the heat to medium and cook, uncovered, for 15–20 minutes or until the sauce is thickened.

Ladle into warm bowls, drizzle with extra whisked yogurt, and sprinkle with chopped cilantro. Serve with lemon wedges for squeezing over the dish, if desired.

For spicy chickpea soup, heat 2 tablespoons sunflower oil in a saucepan, add 1 chopped onion, and cook, stirring, for 1–2 minutes, until softened. Add 1 tablespoon medium or hot curry powder and 2½ cups hot vegetable broth and bring to a boil, then add 1 (15 oz) can chickpeas (garbanzo beans), rinsed and drained, and 1 cup light cream. Bring back to a boil, then reduce the heat to medium and cook for 4–5 minutes or until piping hot. Season, stir in ¼ cup chopped cilantro leaves and serve with crusty bread. **Total cooking time 20 minutes.**

164

spiced fava bean & dill pilaf

Serves **4**
Total cooking time **30 minutes**

2 cups shelled **fava beans**
4 tablespoons **butter**
2 **red chiles**, finely chopped
1 tablespoon **cumin seeds**
2 **whole cloves**
6 **green cardamom pods**
1 **cinnamon stick**
¼ cup **dried red split lentils**, rinsed and drained
1¼ cups **basmati rice** or other **long-grain rice**
6 **scallions**, finely sliced
⅓ cup finely chopped **dill**
salt and **black pepper**

Cook the fava beans in a saucepan of boiling water for 1–2 minutes. Drain, then put into a bowl of cold water and let the beans cool slightly. Drain again, then slip off and discard the skins and set the beans aside.

Melt the butter in a saucepan over low heat, add the red chiles and spices, and stir for 1 minute, then add the lentils and rice and continue to stir until well coated.

Pour over enough water to come about ¾ inch above the level of the rice. Season well and bring to a boil. Stir once, then reduce the heat to low, cover tightly, and cook gently for 8–10 minutes. Remove from the heat and let stand, covered, for 10–12 minutes or until the liquid is absorbed and the rice is tender.

Stir the fava beans, scallions, and dill through the rice, then spoon into a bowls and serve.

For spicy fava bean & dill rice salad, blanch and skin 2⅔ cups shelled fava beans as above. Meanwhile, heat a skillet until hot, add 1 tablespoon cumin seeds, and dry-fry over medium heat until browned, then let cool. Put 2½ cups freshly cooked rice, 2 finely chopped red chiles, the toasted cumin seeds, 6 finely sliced scallions, and the fava beans into a large bowl. Pour ⅔ cup vinaigrette over the salad and sprinkle with a small handful of chopped dill. Season, toss to mix well, and serve. **Total cooking time 10 minutes.**

carrot, pea & potato curry

Serves **4**

Total cooking time **30 minutes**

2 teaspoons **vegetable oil**

3 **whole cloves**

2 **cinnamon sticks**

2 teaspoons **white
poppy seeds**

2 teaspoons **black
peppercorns**

4 **dried red chiles**

1 cup **unsweetened
dried coconut flakes**,
lightly toasted

4 **garlic cloves**, coarsely
chopped

2 **onions**, coarsely chopped

4 teaspoons **sunflower oil**

2 **Yukon Gold** or **white round
potatoes**, peeled and
chopped into 1 inch cubes

2 **large carrots**, peeled and
chopped into 1 inch cubes

1 (14½ oz) **can diced
tomatoes**

1⅓ cups **frozen peas**

salt

mini naans or other
flatbreads, to serve

To make the spice paste, heat the vegetable oil in
a small skillet over medium heat, add the cloves,
cinnamon sticks, poppy seeds, peppercorns, and dried
chiles, and sauté for 1–2 minutes, until fragrant. Put
into a food processor or blender with the coconut,
garlic, and onions and process to a coarse paste.

Heat the sunflower oil in a heavy saucepan, add the
potatoes and carrots, then cover and cook over medium
heat for 2 minutes. Stir in the spice paste and diced
tomatoes and season with salt.

Stir, replace the lid, and simmer for 15–20 minutes or
until the potatoes and carrots are tender, adding the
peas 5 minutes before the end of the cooking time.

Spoon into warm bowls and serve with mini naans or
other flatbreads.

For spicy pea, carrot & potato stir-fry, heat
2 tablespoons olive oil in a large wok until hot, add
2 teaspoons black mustard seeds, and cook over high
heat until the seeds begin to pop. Add 2 teaspoons
cumin seeds, 1 teaspoon ground cumin, 1 teaspoon
ground coriander, 2 teaspoons hot chili powder,
1 (15 oz) can new potatoes, drained and diced,
1 (8¼ oz) can sliced carrots, drained, and 2 cups
frozen peas. Stir-fry over high heat for 4–5 minutes.
Remove from the heat, squeeze the juice of 1 lemon
over the top, and serve. **Total cooking time
10 minutes.**

curried mushrooms & tomatoes

Serves **4**
Total cooking time **20 minutes**

5 tablespoons **sunflower oil**
1 lb **cremini mushrooms,**
  halved or thickly sliced
½ cup **heavy cream**
2 **ripe plum tomatoes,**
  finely chopped
⅓ cup finely chopped **fresh**
  cilantro leaves
salt and **black pepper**
steamed rice, to serve

Spice paste
4 **garlic cloves**, finely chopped
2 teaspoons peeled and finely
  chopped **fresh ginger root**
1 **onion**, finely chopped
1 tablespoon **medium** or **hot**
  curry powder
3 tablespoons **water**

Make the spice paste. Put all the ingredients into a food processor or blender and process until smooth.

Heat 3 tablespoons of the oil in a large wok until hot, add the mushrooms, and stir-fry over high heat for 4–5 minutes. Transfer the contents of the wok to a bowl and wipe out the wok with paper towels.

Heat the remaining oil in the wok until hot, add the curry paste, and stir-fry over medium heat for 3–4 minutes. Return the mushrooms and any juices to the wok, add the cream and tomatoes, and cook, stirring, for 3–4 minutes or until piping hot. Season well.

Remove from the heat, stir in the chopped cilantro, and serve immediately with steamed rice.

For spicy mushroom & tomato stir-fry, heat 2 tablespoons sunflower oil in a large wok or skillet until hot, add 1 lb large sliced cremini mushrooms, 1 tablespoon medium or hot curry powder, 1 teaspoon ginger paste, and 1 teaspoon garlic paste, and stir-fry over high heat for 4–5 minutes. Stir in ½ cup heavy cream and 2 chopped tomatoes and cook for 2–3 minutes or until piping hot. Sprinkle with a handful of chopped cilantro and serve with steamed rice or noodles. **Total cooking time 10 minutes.**

food for
friends

asparagus carbonara

Serves **4**
Total cooking time **10 minutes**

1 tablespoon **olive oil**
2 **scallions**, chopped
12 **fine asparagus spears**
pinch of chopped **tarragon**
1 lb **fresh linguine**
1 **egg**, lightly beaten
¼ cup **crème fraîche** or
   heavy cream
¼ cup grated **Parmesan**
   cheese, plus extra to serve
salt and **black pepper**

Heat the oil in a large skillet. Add the scallions and asparagus and cook for 2–3 minutes, until just cooked through. Stir in the tarragon.

Cook the linguine in a large saucepan of lightly salted boiling water according to the package directions. Drain, reserving a little cooking water, and return to the pan. Add the cooked asparagus and scallions, then add the egg, crème fraîche or heavy cream, and Parmesan. Season and stir together until creamy, adding a little of the pasta cooking water, if needed. Spoon into bowls and sprinkle with more Parmesan to serve.

For poached eggs with asparagus, toss 12 asparagus spears in 2 tablespoons olive oil. Cook on a hot ridged grill pan for 5 minutes, turning frequently, until charred and cooked through. Whisk together 2 tablespoons lemon juice, ¼ cup olive oil, add 1 crushed garlic clove and season. Cut ¼ baguette into small chunks, toss with ⅓ cup olive oil, and bake in a preheated oven, at 400°F, for 7–10 minutes, until golden, then let cool. Poach 4 eggs for 4 minutes for a soft yolk, then pat dry with paper towels. Toss the lemon dressing with ½ bunch (5 oz) spinach and the asparagus. Arrange on plates with the eggs, croutons, and shavings of Parmesan cheese. **Total cooking time 20 minutes.**

174

jeweled fruity spicy pilaf

Serves **4**

Total cooking time **30 minutes**

1 tablespoon **saffron threads**
4 cups **hot vegetable broth**
2 cups **basmati rice** or other
  long-grain rice
1 tablespoon **olive oil**
1 tablespoon **butter**
3 **shallots**, finely chopped
2 **garlic cloves**, finely chopped
4 **cardamom pods**,
  lightly bruised
2 **whole cloves**
2 **cinnamon sticks**
2 teaspoons **cumin seeds**
2 **carrots**, peeled and
  finely diced
¼ cup chopped **dill**
2 cups shelled **soybeans**
⅔ cup **golden raisins**
⅔ cup **dried cranberries**
seeds from 1 **ripe**
  pomegranate
½ cup **slivered pistachio nuts**
salt and **black pepper**

Add the saffron to the hot broth and set aside.

Rinse the rice in cold running water and let drain.

Heat the oil and butter in a heavy saucepan and stir-fry the shallots and garlic for 1–2 minutes over medium heat.

Add the cardamom pods, cloves, cinnamon sticks, cumin seeds, rice, and carrots and stir to mix well. Add the broth mixture along with the dill, season, and bring up to a boil. Stir in the soybeans, golden raisins, and dried cranberries. Cover tightly and reduce the heat to low. Cook for 10–12 minutes without lifting the lid.

Remove from the heat and let stand, undisturbed, for 10 minutes.

Remove the lid (the liquid should have been completely absorbed), stir in the pomegranate seeds and pistachio nuts, and serve immediately.

For fruity spiced couscous, put 3 cups cooked couscous into a wide bowl with 1 finely julienned carrot, 2 finely sliced shallots, ⅔ cup golden raisins, 2 cups chopped fresh dill, and ½ cup pomegranate seeds (from 1 pomegranate). Whisk together ⅓ cup olive oil with the juice of 1 orange and 1 teaspoon each of ground cinnamon and cumin, then pour over the couscous mixture. Season, toss to mix well, and serve. **Total cooking time 10 minutes.**

beet & goat cheese tart

Serves **4–6**
Total cooking time **30 minutes**

2 tablespoons **olive oil**
2 **garlic cloves**, chopped
1 teaspoon **thyme leaves**
2 tablespoons **balsamic vinegar**
10 **cooked beets** (not pickled), sliced or cut into thin wedges
flour, for dusting
1 sheet **ready-to-bake puff pastry**, chilled
4 oz **crumbly goat cheese**
thyme or **snipped chives**, to garnish

Put the oil into an ovenproof skillet over medium-low heat and, when hot, sauté the garlic and thyme for 1–2 minutes, until just softened. Pour in the vinegar and simmer gently for 1–2 minutes, until just sticky.

Arrange the beets to fit snugly and attractively in the pan, then increase the heat slightly and cook for 4–5 minutes, until the underside begins to brown.

Meanwhile, place the pastry on a lightly floured work surface and roll into a circle about ½ inch larger than the pan.

Lay the pastry over the pan, tucking the edges in neatly to cover the beets, and bake in a preheated oven, at 400°F, for 15–20 minutes, until the pastry is puffed and golden.

Invert the tart onto a large plate, then crumble the goat cheese over the top and serve garnished with the thyme or chives.

For individual goat cheese & beet quiches, unroll a sheet of chilled, store-bought rolled dough pie crust and use to line 4 greased, individual tart pans. Fill the pastry shells with 4 diced, cooked beets, ⅔ cup defrosted peas, and 4 oz crumbled goat cheese. Break 3 eggs into a bowl, beat together, then mix in 3 tablespoons light cream and 1 teaspoon chopped thyme leaves. Pour into the filled shells and bake in a preheated oven, at 425°F, for 12–15 minutes, or until set and golden. **Total cooking time 20 minutes.**

mushroom risotto

Serves **4**
Total cooking time **30 minutes**

½ oz **dried porcini**
1 cup **boiling water**
1 tablespoon **olive oil**
2 **shallots**, diced
1½ cups **risotto rice**
⅔ cup **white wine**
2½ cups **hot vegetable broth**
6 oz **cremini mushrooms**
1 teaspoon chopped **thyme**
salt and **black pepper**
2 tablespoons grated
   Parmesan cheese, to serve

Put the dried porcini into a bowl and cover with the measured water. Let stand for 15 minutes.

Meanwhile, heat the olive oil in a saucepan and sauté the shallots for 2–3 minutes, unitl softened but not browned.

Stir in the rice and continue to stir, until the edges of the grains look translucent.

Pour in the wine, and cook for 1–2 minutes over high heat and stir until it is absorbed.

Add a ladle of the hot broth, reduce the heat to medium, and stir continuously until it has been absorbed. Repeat with the remaining hot broth, a ladle at a time.

Drain the porcini, reserving the liquid. Coarsely chop the porcini and add to the rice with the fresh mushrooms and a ladle of the porcini liquid.

Continue to stir and add liquid, until the rice is "al dente."

Stir in the thyme, season, and serve sprinkled with grated Parmesan.

For quick mushroom rice, heat 2 tablespoons olive oil in a skillet and sauté 12 oz cremini mushrooms and 4 sliced scallions for 5–6 minutes. Stir in 2 cups cooked rice and 1 tablespoon chopped parsley. Season and serve sprinkled with 2 tablespoons grated Parmesan cheese. **Total cooking time 10 minutes.**

watercress, raisins & pine nut fusilli

Serves **4**
Total cooking time **10 minutes**

1 lb **fusilli**
2 tablespoons **olive oil**
8 cups coarsely chopped
   watercress or other **peppery**
   greens (about 8 oz)
⅓ cup **raisins**
½ cup **toasted pine nuts**
grated zest of 1 **lemon**
Parmesan cheese shavings,
   to serve

Cook the fusilli in a saucepan of boiling water according to the package directions, until "al dente."

Meanwhile, heat the olive oil in a large saucepan and add the watercress or other peppery greens. Stir until wilted and then add the raisins.

Drain the pasta and add to the greens and raisins. Add the pine nuts and lemon zest, then toss together.

Serve sprinkled with Parmesan shavings.

For fusilli & watercress salad, cook 12 oz fusilli in a saucepan of boiling water according to the package directions, until "al dente." Drain and refresh under cold water. Mix the pasta together with 2 carrots, 2 zucchini, and 1 cored and seeded red bell pepper, which have all been cut into matchsticks. Add 3 cups watercress or other peppery greens. Whisk together 3 tablespoons extra-virgin olive oil, 1 tablespoon sherry vinegar, 1 crushed garlic clove, ½ teaspoon mustard, and ½ teaspoon honey. Drizzle the dressing over the salad and serve sprinkled with 2 tablespoons toasted pine nuts. **Total cooking time 20 minutes.**

herbed mushrooms with grits

Serves **4**
Total cooking time **30 minutes**

1 cup **instant grits** or **polenta**
1 tablespoon finely chopped
   rosemary leaves
1 tablespoon finely chopped
   sage leaves
½ cup finely chopped
   flat leaf parsley
1 stick (4 oz) **butter**
6½ cups **hot vegetable broth**
1½ lb) large **Portobello
   mushrooms**, thickly sliced
3 **garlic cloves**, crushed
½ cup **cream cheese with
   garlic and herbs**
½ teaspoon **dried red
   pepper flakes**
salt and **black pepper**

Put the grits or polenta, rosemary, sage, half the parsley, and half the butter into a saucepan over medium heat and gradually whisk in the broth, stirring continuously.

Reduce the heat to low, season well, and cook, stirring constantly, according to the package directions, until the grains becomes thick and starts bubbling. Remove from the heat and keep warm.

Meanwhile, heat the remaining butter in a large, nonstick skillet over high heat. Add the mushrooms and garlic and stir-fry for 6–8 minutes. Season well and stir in the cream cheese and dried chile. Stir-fry for 2–3 minutes, until bubbling. Remove from the heat and stir in the remaining parsley.

Serve immediately on warm plates over the grains.

For creamy mushroom & herb pasta, cook 12 oz quick-cooking pasta according to the package directions. Meanwhile, heat a large skillet over high heat and add 2 tablespoons butter, 2 finely chopped garlic cloves, and 1½ lb thinly sliced Portobello mushrooms. Stir-fry over high heat for 3–4 minutes, then stir in 1 cup cream cheese with garlic and herbs. Season, toss to mix well, and stir in 3 tablespoons chopped flat leaf parsley. Serve over the pasta. **Total cooking time 10 minutes.**

baked asparagus alfredo crepes

Serves **4**

Total cooking time **30 minutes**

1½ lb **asparagus**, woody
ends trimmed

3 tablespoons **olive oil**

1 (16 oz) jar **alfredo sauce**

freshly **grated nutmeg**,
to taste

12 **cooked crepes** (prepared
from a box of pancake mix,
following package directions)

freshly grated **Parmesan
cheese**, to sprinkle

Put the asparagus into a roasting pan, toss with the oil, and roast in a preheated oven, at 475°F, for 7 minutes or until tender. Set aside.

Reduce the oven temperature to 425°F.

Season the the alfredo sauce with nutmeg. Spread a little sauce onto a cooked crepe and top with some asparagus. Roll up and put into a 2-quart ovenproof dish. Repeat with the remaining crepes and asparagus.

Drizzle the remaining sauce over the pancakes in the dish, then sprinkle with the Parmesan and and grate over some nutmeg. Bake for 12–15 minutes or until golden. Serve immediately.

For broiled asparagus bruschettas with melted cheese, blanch 1¼ lb asparagus tips in a saucepan of lightly salted boiling water for 2–3 minutes. Drain and divide the asparagus among 8 slices of toasted sourdough bread and sprinkle with 1¾ cups shredded fontina, Gruyère, or Swiss cheese. Broil under a preheated medium broiler for 2–3 minutes or until the cheese has just melted. Season and serve with a crisp green salad. **Total cooking time 10 minutes.**

spicy tofu & mushroom stir-fry

Serves **4**
Total cooking time **10 minutes**

2 tablespoons **vegetable oil**
8 oz **shiitake mushrooms**,
  halved if large
1 **leek** (white only), thinly
  sliced
2 **garlic cloves**, chopped
2 teaspoons grated **fresh
  ginger root**
3 tablespoons **black bean
  sauce**
1 teaspoon **chili sauce**
pinch of **ground Sichuan
  pepper**
1 tablespoon **cornstarch**
⅔ cup **vegetable broth**
2 tablespoons **soy sauce**
1 tablespoon **rice wine
  vinegar**
1 tablespoon **sugar**
¾ (16 oz) package **firm tofu**,
  drained and cubed
2 **scallions**, shredded
plain boiled rice, to serve

Heat the oil in a large wok, add the mushrooms, and cook for 2 minutes. Add the leek and cook for 2 minutes, until softened. Stir in the garlic and ginger, followed by the black bean and chili sauces and the Sichuan pepper.

Mix together the cornstarch, broth, soy sauce, vinegar, and sugar and add to the wok. Carefully stir in the tofu. Let simmer for 2–3 minutes, until the sauce has thickened. Sprinkle with the scallions and serve with plain boiled rice.

For egg-fried tofu & shiitake rice, boil 1¼ cups rice according to package directions, then drain. Heat 2 tablespoons oil in a wok, add ¼ (16 oz) package firm tofu, drained and cubed, and cook for 3 minutes. Remove from the wok. Add 5 oz shiitake mushrooms. Cook for 2 minutes, then add 2 chopped garlic cloves, 1 teaspoon grated fresh ginger root, and 2 chopped scallions. Cook for 1 minute. Crack 1 egg into the wok and stir until just cooked. Add the rice, tofu, ⅓ cup defrosted frozen peas, and 3 tablespoons soy sauce, stir, and serve. **Total cooking time 20 minutes.**

spicy butternut risotto with ricotta

Serves **4**
Total cooking time **30 minutes**

4 tablespoons **butter**
1 tablespoon **olive oil**
1 **onion**, finely chopped
½ **butternut squash**, peeled, seeded, and chopped
1 **red chile,** seeded and finely chopped
1½ cups **risotto rice**
½ cup **dry white wine**
3 cups **hot vegetable broth**
½ cup grated **Parmesan cheese**
3 **sage leaves**, finely chopped
¼ cup **ricotta cheese**
salt and **black pepper**

Heat half the butter with the oil in a large saucepan, add the onion, and sauté for 5 minutes, until softened. Add the squash and cook for an additional 2 minutes. Stir most of the chile into the pan along with the rice and cook for 2 minutes, until the rice is well coated.

Pour the wine into the pan and cook until it has simmered away. Gradually stir in the hot broth, a little at a time, stirring frequently and letting the rice absorb the broth before adding more. When the rice is soft, after about 15 minutes, stir in the remaining butter and the Parmesan and season. Spoon into serving bowls, sprinkle with the sage, ricotta, and remaining chile, and serve.

For spicy butternut & ricotta gnocchi, cook ½ butternut squash, peeled, seeded, and chopped, in a large saucepan of lightly salted boiling water for 3 minutes. Add 1 (16 oz) package fresh gnocchi and cook according to the package directions. Drain and toss through 2 finely chopped sage leaves, ½ teaspoon dried red pepper flakes, and 2 tablespoons butter. Season, then spoon onto serving plates and top with dollops of ricotta and some grated Parmesan cheese. **Total cooking time 10 minutes.**

green lentil stew with garlic bread

Serves **4**
Total cooking time **30 minutes**

¼ cup **olive oil**
1 **red bell pepper**, cored,
seeded, and cut into chunks
1 **green bell pepper**, cored,
seeded, and cut into chunks
1 **red onion**, coarsely chopped
1 **garlic clove**, sliced
1 **fennel bulb**, trimmed
and sliced
1¼ cups **dried green lentils**,
rinsed
2½ cups **vegetable broth**
1¼ cups **red wine**

Garlic bread
4 tablespoons **butter**,
softened
1 **garlic clove**, crushed
2 tablespoons coarsely
chopped **thyme**
1 **whole wheat French
baguette** or **long
Italian bread**
salt and **black pepper**

Heat the oil in a large, heavy saucepan and cook the bell peppers, onion, garlic, and fennel over medium-high heat, stirring frequently, for 5 minutes, until softened and lightly browned. Stir in the dried lentils, broth, and wine and bring to a boil, then reduce the heat and let simmer for 25 minutes, until the lentils are tender.

Meanwhile, beat the softened butter with the garlic and thyme in a bowl and season with a little salt and black pepper. Cut the bread into thick slices, almost all the way through but leaving the bottom attached. Spread the butter thickly over each slice, then wrap the bread in aluminum foil and place in a preheated oven, at 400°F, for 15 minutes.

Serve the stew hot, ladled into warm serving bowls, with the torn hot garlic and herb bread on the side for mopping up the juices.

For green lentil & sun-dried tomato salad, put 1 cup rinsed dried green lentils into a saucepan, cover generously with cold water, and bring to a boil. Reduce the heat and simmer for 15 minutes, until just tender. Drain, then toss with the juice of 1 lemon, 1 crushed garlic clove, and ¼ cup olive oil, and season with salt and black pepper. Stir 1 (8½ oz) jar sun-dried tomatoes, drained, 1 small finely chopped red onion, and a handful of chopped flat leaf parsley through the lentils and serve with some arugula. **Total cooking time 20 minutes.**

herbed tomato & cheese tart

Serves **4**
Total cooking time **30 minutes**

1 sheet chilled **ready-to-bake buff pastry**
3–4 tablespoons **black olive tapenade** or **Dijon mustard**
5 **ripe plum tomatoes**, finely sliced
8 large **basil leaves**, coarsely torn
4 oz **Camembert cheese**
4 oz **goat cheese**
2 tablespoons **thyme**, plus extra to garnish
1–2 tablespoons **extra virgin olive oil**
salt and **black pepper**

Roll out the pastry and use it to line a 10 inch tart pan.

Spread the tapenade or Dijon mustard over the bottom of the tart.

Lay the tomato slices in concentric circles in the tart, discarding any juice or seeds that have run from them. Season the tomatoes (keeping in mind that tapenade is salty) and sprinkle with the basil.

Cut the Camembert and goat cheese into thin wedges or slices, according to its shape. Arrange a circle of Camembert pieces around the outside and a circle of goat cheese within. Put any remaining pieces of cheese in the middle.

Sprinkle with the thyme and drizzle the olive oil on top.

Bake in a preheated oven, at 400˚F, for 15–18 minutes, until the pastry is cooked and the cheese is golden and bubbling. Serve immediately, garnished with thyme.

For fresh tomato & two cheese pasta, cook 12 oz farfalle pasta according to the package directions. Meanwhile, finely chop 4 plum tomatoes, 1 cup pitted black ripe olives, 1 cup basil, and 2 tablespoons thyme and put into a bowl with 4 oz each of diced goat cheese and Camembert cheese. Drain the pasta and add to the tomato mixture. Season, toss to mix well, and serve immediately. **Total cooking time 20 minutes.**

eggplant with cucumber noodles

Serves **4**
Total cooking time **20 minutes**

12 **baby eggplants**, halved
¼ cup **white miso paste**
3 tablespoons **rice wine vinegar**
2 tablespoons **sugar**
1 tablespoon **sake** or **water**
1 tablespoon **sesame seeds**
1 cup **soybeans**
10 oz **cooked rice noodles**
½ **cucumber**, thinly sliced
2 **scallions**, thinly sliced
salt

Make a crisscross pattern on the cut sides of the eggplants and place them, cut side down, on a broiler pan. Cook for 7–10 minutes under a preheated hot broiler until charred. Mix together the miso paste, 2 tablespoons of the vinegar, the sugar, and sake or water. Turn the eggplants over and brush with the miso mixture. Return to the broiler for 3–5 minutes, until the eggplant is soft, then sprinkle with the sesame seeds and cook for an additional 1 minute.

Meanwhile, cook the soybeans in a saucepan of lightly salted boiling water for 2 minutes, until soft. Drain and cool under cold running water. Toss the beans together with the noodles, cucumber, scallions, the remaining vinegar, and season with salt. Serve with the broiled eggplant.

For broiled eggplant salad with miso ginger dressing, cut 2 large eggplants into thin slices and toss together with ⅓ cup vegetable oil. Cook on a hot ridged grill pan for 2–3 minutes on each side, until charred and soft. Mix together 1 tablespoon white miso paste with 2 tablespoons rice wine vinegar, a pinch of sugar, 2 teaspoons grated fresh ginger root, and ½ finely chopped red chile. Whisk in ⅓ cup vegetable oil, then toss together with the grilled eggplant and 7 cups arugula. **Total cooking time 10 minutes.**

lima bean & vegetable gratin

Serves **4**
Total cooking time **30 minutes**

6 tablespoons **butter**, chilled
  and diced
⅓ cups **all-purpose flour**
1 cup chopped **walnuts**
½ cup shredded **cheddar
  cheese**
1 (16 oz) package **peas,
  cauliflower**, and **carrots**,
  thawed if frozen
1 (16 oz) **jar tomato and
  herb sauce**
2 **garlic cloves**, crushed
⅓ cup finely chopped **basil**
1 (15 oz) **can lima beans**,
  drained and rinsed
salt and **black pepper**

Rub the butter into the all-purpose flour until crumbs form. Stir in the chopped walnuts and shredded cheese, season and set aside.

Cook the carrots, peas, and cauliflower in a saucepan of boiling water for 1–2 minutes, then drain.

Meanwhile, heat the tomato and herb sauce in a large saucepan until bubbling.

Stir in the garlic, basil, lima beans, and blanched vegetables. Transfer to a medium ovenproof dish and sprinkle with the crumb topping. Bake in a preheated oven, at 400°F, for 15–20 minutes or until golden and bubbling.

For lima bean & walnut pâté, put 2 (15 oz) cans lima beans, rinsed and drained, and the juice and finely grated zest of 1 lemon into a blender or food processor with 1 crushed garlic clove, ¼ cup each of finely chopped basil and mint, ½ cup chopped walnuts, ½ cup mayonnaise, and 2 teaspoons Dijon mustard. Process until fairly smooth and serve spread thickly on toasted sourdough bread with a salad. **Total cooking time 10 minutes.**

leek & blue cheese tart

Serves **4**

Total cooking time **30 minutes**

5 oz small **baby leeks**, trimmed

1 sheet chilled **ready-to-bake puff pastry**

oil, for greasing

1 **egg**, beaten

⅓ cup **mascarpone cheese**

4 oz **blue cheese**

salt and **black pepper**

Cook the leeks in a saucepan of lightly salted boiling water for 1 minute, until just soft. Drain and cool under cold running water.

Unwrap the pastry a place on a lightly greased baking sheet. Use a sharp knife to lightly score a ½ inch border all around the pastry, being careful not to cut all the way through. Lightly prick the inside of the pastry with the end of a fork and brush all over the border with egg.

Mix together the remaining egg, the mascarpone, and half the blue cheese, then spread the mixture over the pastry. Arrange the leeks on top and sprinkle with the remaining cheese. Cook in a preheated oven, at 400˚F, for 20 minutes, until the pastry is golden and cooked through.

For creamy leek & blue cheese pasta, cut 2 large leeks into thin slices. Cook in a large saucepan of lightly salted boiling water for 3–5 minutes, until soft, together with 1 lb fresh penne, cooked according to the package directions. Drain, reserving a little of the cooking water. Return to the pan and stir in ⅓ cup crème fraîche or heavy cream, adding a little of the cooking water, if needed, and crumble 4 oz blue cheese over the top. Sprinkle with some chopped parsley before serving. **Total cooking time 10 minutes.**

deep-fried halloumi fritters

Serves **4**

Total cooking time **20 minutes**

2 cups **all-purpose flour**

1 **egg**, separated

1 ¼ cups **ice-cold lager**

½ **ice-cold water**

vegetable oil, for deep-frying

1 lb **halloumi**, **mozzarella**,
   or **Muenster cheese**

To serve

arugula

lemon wedges

Sift the flour into a large bowl and add the egg yolk. Gradually whisk in the lager, then add the measured water and whisk until well combined.

Whisk the egg white in a separate bowl until stiff peaks form. Fold this into the batter.

Fill a deep fryer or a large, deep, heavy saucepan two-thirds full with vegetable oil. Heat the oil to 350°F or until a cube of bread turns golden in 10–15 seconds.

Cut the cheese into ½ inch slices, then dip in the batter to coat. Fry the cheese, in batches, for 3–4 minutes, or until crisp and golden brown. Remove with a slotted spoon, season, and serve on arugula with wedges of lemon to squeeze over the cheese.

For mixed bell pepper & halloumi skewers, cut 2 seeded red bell peppers and 2 seeded yellow bell peppers, 2 red onions, and 10 oz halloumi or Muenster cheese into bite-size pieces. Put the vegetables and cheese into a wide bowl. Mix together 2 crushed garlic cloves, ½ cup olive oil, 2 teaspoons dried thyme, and the juice and finely grated zest of 1 lemon. Pour the dressing over the cheese and vegetables and toss to mix. Thread the vegetables and cheese alternately onto 12 metal skewers. Season and broil under a preheated medium–high broiler for 4–5 minutes on each side. Serve immediately. **Total cooking time 10 minutes.**

tagliatelle in blue cheese & walnuts

Serves **4**
Total cooking time **10 minutes**

1 lb **tagliatelle**
1 cup **light cream**
8 oz **Gorgonzola dolce**, or
   other **blue cheese**, crumbled
1 cup **walnut pieces**, toasted
2 tablespoons shredded **basil**

Cook the pasta in a large saucepan of boiling water for 8–9 minutes, or according to the package directions.

Meanwhile, put the light cream into a skillet with the blue cheese over medium-low heat. When the cheese is melted, stir in the walnuts.

Drain the pasta and toss in the creamy cheese and walnut sauce.

Serve in warm bowls, sprinkled with the shredded basil.

For blue cheese & walnut tortilla pizza, wilt 1 (12 oz) package baby spinach leaves in a saucepan with 1 tablespoon olive oil. Heat 2 tortillas according to the package directions. Place the tortillas on baking sheets and spread with ¾ cup canned diced tomatoes. Sprinkle with 8 oz crumbled Gorgonzola dolce or other blue cheese and 1 cup toasted walnut pieces. Toast under a preheated hot broiler for 3–4 minutes, until bubbling and golden. **Total cooking time 10 minutes.**

roasted roots & feta pearl barley

Serves **4**

Total cooking time **30 minutes**

2 **red onions**, cut into thin
    wedges
16 **carrots**, scrubbed and
    cut into chunks
4 **raw beets**, peeled and cut
    into thin wedges
2–3 tablespoons **olive oil**
1½ teaspoons **cumin seeds**
1½ teaspoons **ground
    coriander**
1½ **vegetable bouillon cubes**
1⅓ cups **pearl barley**
2 cups crumbled **feta cheese**
⅓ cup **fresh cilantro leaves**

Put all the prepared vegetables into a large roasting pan, drizzle with the oil, and toss to coat. Add the cumin seeds and ground coriander and toss again. Put into the top of a preheated oven, at 425°F, for 20–25 minutes, until the vegetables are tender and lightly charred.

Meanwhile, bring a large saucepan of lightly salted water to a boil, add the bouillon cubes and pearl barley, and cook for 20 minutes, until the grain is tender. Drain, then toss with the vegetables. Add the crumbled feta and cilantro leaves, toss well, and serve.

For carrot, beet & feta gratin, heat 3 tablespoons olive oil in a large skillet, add 1 large, thinly sliced red onion, 8 peeled and sliced carrots, and 4 raw beets, peeled and cut into thin wedges, and cook for 8–10 minutes, until tender and cooked through. Add 1½ teaspoons cumin seeds and ¾ teaspoon ground coriander, then toss and cook for an additional 2 minutes. Divide among 4 small gratin dishes, then sprinkle 2 cups crumbled feta cheese over the tops. Cook under a preheated hot broiler for 2–3 minutes, until the feta has turned golden in places. Serve with warm crusty bread. **Total cooking time 20 minutes.**

creamy walnut & arugula pasta

Serves **4**
Total cooking time **15 minutes**

1 lb **orecchiette**
1 cup **walnut pieces**
1 **garlic clove**, crushed
¼ cup **extra virgin olive oil**
⅓ cup **heavy cream**
½ cup grated **Parmesan cheese**
4 cups **arugula**
salt and **black pepper**

Cook the orecchiette in a large saucepan of lightly salted boiling water according to the package directions.

Meanwhile, put most of the walnuts, the garlic, oil, cream, and grated Parmesan into a blender or food processor and process until smooth. Season.

Drain the pasta, reserving a little of the cooking water, then stir through the walnut sauce, adding a little cooking water, if needed. Toss in the arugula and transfer to serving bowls. Top with the reserved walnuts and serve immediately.

For pasta with goat cheese & walnut sauce, mix 1 crushed garlic clove with 3 oz soft goat cheese, ⅓ cup cream cheese, ¼ cup chopped walnuts, and a large handful of chopped basil. Season. Cook 1 lb fresh pasta in a large saucepan of lightly salted boiling water according to the package directions. Drain, reserving a little of the cooking water. Return to the pan and stir through the sauce, adding a little cooking water, if needed. Top with more basil and sprinkle with some extra goat cheese to serve. **Total cooking time 10 minutes.**

desserts

mango and raspberry gratin

Serves **4**
Total cooking time **10 minutes**

½ cup **heavy cream**
⅔ cup **mascarpone cheese**
1 cup **canned** or **freshly prepared custard** or **vanilla pudding and pie filling**
1 **mango**, peeled, pitted, and sliced
2 cups **raspberries**

Whip the cream until soft peaks form, then carefully stir together with the mascarpone and custard or vanilla pudding and pie filling.

Put the mango and raspberries into a small, shallow ovenproof dish and spread the cream mixture on top. Cook on a top shelf in a hot broiler for 2–3 minutes, until lightly browned.

For mango cakes with raspberry sauce, butter 4 individual ramekins or custard cups. Mix together 2 tablespoons each softened butter and packed light brown sugar and spoon the mixture into the bottom of the ramekins. Add 1 tablespoon chopped mango to each ramekin. Mix together 1 stick (4 oz) softened butter, ½ cup granulated sugar, ¾ cup all-purpose flour, and ¾ teaspoon baking powder with 2 eggs and 1 teaspoon vanilla extract until a smooth batter forms. Spoon the batter into the ramekins and cook in a preheated oven, at 350°F, for 20–25 minutes, until just cooked through. Press 1 cup raspberries through a strainer and sift in 1 tablespoon confectioners' sugar to make a sauce. Spoon the sauce over the cakes to serve. **Total cooking time 30 minutes.**

apple, maple & pecan whips

Serves **4**
Total cooking time **10 minutes**

¾ cup **good-quality
   applesauce**
1 **Granny Smith apple,**
   peeled and grated or finely
   chopped
1 cup **heavy cream**
1 cup **freshly prepared
   custard** or **vanilla pudding**
3 tablespoons **maple syrup**
¼ cup **pecans,** toasted and
   chopped
cookies, to serve

Put the applesauce and chopped apple into a small saucepan, cook for 5 minutes to soften, then put into metal bowl in the freezer for a few minutes to cool.

Whip the cream until soft peaks form, then stir in the custard or vanilla pudding. Swirl through the apple puree and maple syrup, then spoon into serving dishes. Top with toasted pecans and serve with cookies.

For apple & pecan brioches, core and thinly slice 2 Braeburn apples, arrange on a baking sheet, and brush over a little melted butter. Cook under a preheated medium broiler for 3 minutes on each side until lightly golden. Mix ⅔ cup each of milk and cream with 1 egg and 1 teaspoon vanilla extract. Dip 8 slices of brioche in the mixture until well coated. Heat a little butter in a nonstick skillet and cook the brioche, in batches, for 2–3 minutes on each side until golden. Arrange the apple slices on top, add spoonfuls of crème fraîche or Greek yogurt, and sprinkle with chopped pecans. Drizzle with a little maple syrup to serve. **Total cooking time 20 minutes.**

iced berries with white chocolate

Serves **4**
Total cooking time **10 minutes**

¾ cup **heavy cream**
6 oz **white chocolate**,
   chopped
½ teaspoon **vanilla extract**
1 (1 lb) package **frozen
   mixed berries**

Put the cream into a small saucepan and heat until boiling. Remove from the heat and stir in the chocolate and vanilla extract and mix until melted.

Arrange the berries in chilled serving bowls, drizzle with the sauce, and serve.

For white chocolate berry mousses, melt 6 oz chopped white chocolate in a heatproof bowl set over a saucepan of simmering water and let cool a little. Beat 1 cup cream cheese and mix in 1 cup heavy cream until smooth. Stir in the cooled chocolate. In a separate bowl, whisk 3 eggs with ⅔ cup superfine sugar until light and fluffy. Fold into the cream cheese mixture, one-third at a time. Place a handful of mixed berries in 4 serving dishes, spoon over some of the cream mixture, followed by some more berries. Keep layering and finish with shavings of white chocolate. **Total cooking time 20 minutes.**

toasted ginger syrup waffles

Serves **4**
Total cooking time **10 minutes**

4 tablespoons **butter**
¼ cup **heavy cream**
2 tablespoons packed
  dark brown sugar
1 piece **preserved ginger**,
  drained and finely chopped
2 tablespoons **preserved
  ginger syrup**
8 **Belgian-style waffles**
vanilla ice cream, to serve

Put the butter into a small saucepan with the cream, sugar, preserved ginger, and syrup. Warm over low heat for 5–6 minutes, stirring occasionally, until the butter has melted and the sugar dissolved.

Meanwhile, toast the waffles according to the package directions and arrange on serving plates. Top with a scoop of ice cream and serve warm, drizzled with the ginger syrup.

For ginger syrup pain perdu, prepare the ginger syrup as in the recipe above. Meanwhile, put 2 eggs into a large, shallow bowl with ½ cup superfine sugar and 1 cup milk and whisk until smooth. Dip 4 slices of slightly stale brioche into the mixture, turning to coat both sides. Melt 6 tablespoons unsalted butter in a large, nonstick skillet and cook the brioche over medium-low heat for 4–5 minutes, turning once, until golden. Arrange on plates and top with a scoop of vanilla ice cream, a dusting of confectioners' sugar, and a drizzle of the ginger syrup. **Total cooking time 20 minutes.**

baked honeyed figs & raspberries

Serves **4**
Total cooking time **20 minutes**

8 **figs**, quartered
1 cup **raspberries**
¼ cup **honey**
finely grated zest of
   1 medium **orange**
coconut ice cream, to serve

Cut 4 large squares of aluminum foil. Divide the figs and raspberries among the pieces of foil, drizzle with the honey, and sprinkle with the orange zest.

Bring the edges of the foil up to the center and twist to form packages. Place on a large baking sheet and bake in a preheated oven, at 400°F, for 15 minutes.

Open the packages and serve the fruit and juices with spoonfuls of coconut ice cream.

For fig, raspberry & honey yogurt desserts,
crumble 8 gingersnaps and spoon into 4 glasses. Divide 4 chopped figs and 1 cup raspberries among the glasses and drizzle each with honey. Spoon 3 tablespoons coconut yogurt over each and serve each topped with a raspberry. **Total cooking time 10 minutes.**

orange & strawberry salad

Serves **4**
Total cooking time **10 minutes**

⅓ cup **granulated sugar**
½ cup **water**
1 tablespoon thinly sliced **basil**
1 cup hulled and halved
   strawberries
4 **oranges**

Put the sugar and measured water into a saucepan and bring to a boil. Simmer for 2–3 minutes, then let cool briefly before adding the basil.

Put the strawberries into a bowl. Peel and segment 4 oranges over the bowl to catch the juice. Add the orange segments to the strawberries.

Pour in the sugar syrup and serve.

For caramelized oranges, peel 4 oranges, then slice them thinly. Put into a shallow serving dish and pour over 1 tablespoon orange liqueur. Put ½ cup granulated sugar, 1 cinnamon stick, and ⅔ cup water into a saucepan. Heat, stirring, until the sugar has dissolved. Continue to simmer until the sugar starts to caramelize and turns a rich caramel color. Pour the syrup over the oranges. Decorate with ¼ cup toasted pine nuts and 1 tablespoon chopped mint. **Total cooking time 20 minutes.**

lemon puddings

Serves **4**
Total cooking time **30 minutes**

4 tablespoons **butter**
⅔ cup **superfine sugar**
  or **granulated sugar**
2 **eggs**, separated
⅓ cup **all-purpose flour**
⅔ cup **milk**
⅔ cup **light cream**
finely grated zest of **1 lemon**
  and juice of ½ lemon
confectioners' sugar, to serve

Put the butter and superfine or granulated sugar into a bowl and beat with a handheld electric mixer until pale and creamy. Add the egg yolks and mix in well, then stir in the flour. Gradually whisk in the milk and cream, followed by the lemon zest and juice.

Whisk the egg whites until stiff peaks form. Stir one-third of the whites into the batter. Then carefully fold in the remainder, half at a time. Spoon the mixture into 4 individual ramekins and bake in a preheated oven, at 350°F, for 15 minutes or until golden. Dust with confectioners' sugar to serve.

For lemon mousse, using a handheld electric mixer, mix together 1 ¼ cups heavy cream, ⅓ cup superfine sugar, and the finely grated zest of 1 lemon. Stir in 1 tablespoon lemon juice or to taste and whisk until smooth. Whisk 2 egg whites until stiff peaks form. Stir a spoonful of the mixture into the whipped cream, then carefully fold in the remainder, half at a time. Spoon into serving bowls and grate over some more lemon zest to serve. **Total cooking time 20 minutes.**

warm chocolate cherry tarts

Serves **4**
Total cooking time **20 minutes**

8 oz **semisweet chocolate**,
  broken into pieces
3 tablespoons **heavy cream**
1 tablespoon **brandy**
2 **eggs** and 1 **egg yolk**
¼ cup **superfine sugar** or
  granulated sugar
¼ cup **undyed candied**
  cherries, halved
4 **store-bought individual**
  pie crusts

Put the chocolate, cream, and brandy into a small heatproof bowl. Set it over a saucepan of gently simmering water, so the bottom of the bowl is not touching the water, and heat for a couple of minutes, until the chocolate is melted. Let cool a little.

Whisk together the eggs, egg yolk, and sugar with a handheld electric mixer until pale and creamy. Carefully stir the chocolate mixture into the eggs. Arrange the cherries in the pie crusts, pour the chocolate mixture over them, and bake in a preheated oven, at 375°F, for 12 minutes or until just set.

For cherries with chocolate dipping sauce,
heat 1 cup heavy cream in a saucepan until boiling. Put 8 oz chopped semisweet chocolate into a bowl. Pour the cream over the chocolate and stir until smooth. Add a splash of brandy or kirsch, if desired. Place in a warm serving bowl and serve with fresh cherries for dunking. **Total cooking time 10 minutes.**

226

blueberry & banana french toast

Serves **4**
Total cooking time **20 minutes**

2 **eggs**
¼ cup **milk**
4 teaspoons **sugar**
4 slices of **stale white bread**
4 tablespoons **butter**
½ cup **blueberries**
2 **bananas**, sliced

To serve
ice cream
maple syrup

Beat together the eggs, milk, and 2 teaspoons of the sugar in a bowl. Pour into a shallow dish and dip both sides of the bread slices into the egg mixture.

Heat the butter in a large skillet, add the bread (you might need to cook 1 or 2 slices at a time), and cook for 2 minutes on each side, until crisp and golden. Sprinkle with the remaining sugar.

Cut the French toasts in half diagonally and sprinkle with the blueberries and banana slices. Serve with ice cream and a drizzle of maple syrup.

For blueberry pancakes with banana, put ⅔ cup all-purpose flour, ½ teaspoon baking powder, 1 tablespoon sugar, 1 egg, and ⅓ cup milk into a food processor or blender and process together to make a smooth, thick batter. Stir in ¼ cup blueberries. Heat 1 tablespoon sunflower oil in a large skillet, add 2 large spoonfuls of the batter, and cook for 1–2 minutes on each side, until golden. Repeat with the remaining batter to make another 2 pancakes. Serve warm with sliced banana and a drizzle of honey. **Total cooking time 10 minutes.**

sambuca watermelon & pineapple

Serves **4**
Total cooking time **10 minutes**

½ small **watermelon**
1 small **pineapple**
4 shots of **Sambuca**
2 tablespoons **toasted
    slivered almonds**
4 scoops of **vanilla ice cream,**
    to serve

Peel the watermelon and pineapple and cut into
½ inch thick slices.

Stack the slices on top of each other on 4 serving
plates, alternating the fruits.

Pour 1 shot of the Sambuca over each, sprinkle with
the slivered almonds, and serve with a scoop of vanilla
ice cream.

For pineapple fritters, sift 1⅔ cups all-purpose flour
into a bowl, then whisk in ½ cup warm water, ½ cup
beer, ½ tablespoon vegetable oil, and ½ tablespoon
marsala or other sweet red wine to make a batter.
Cut 1 large and peeled cored pineapple into thick slices.
Pour sunflower oil into a deep fryer or large saucepan
and heat to 350–375°F, or until a cube of bread
dropped into the oil browns in 30 seconds. Whisk
2 egg whites into the batter and then dip in the
pineapple slices, shaking off any excess. Working in
batches, if necessary, carefully drop into the hot oil.
Deep-fry for 3–4 minutes, until golden all over. Remove
with a slotted spoon and drain on paper towels. Serve
sprinkled with torn mint and dusted with confectioenrs'
sugar. **Total cooking time 30 minutes.**

cherry & vanilla brûlée

Serves **4**
Total cooking time **10 minutes**

2 cups pitted **ripe cherries**,
coarsely chopped
¾ cup **superfine sugar**
or **granulated sugar**
¼ cup **candied cherries**,
coarsely chopped
¼ cup **kirsch or cherry
liqueur**
1¾ cups **vanilla yogurt**

Mix the fresh cherries in a bowl with the half the sugar, the chopped candied cherries, and kirsch.

Spoon the cherry mixture into 4 glass dessert bowls and top with the yogurt.

Sprinkle the remaining sugar over the yogurt and use a chef's torch (or place the ramekins under a preheated hot broiler for 2–3 minutes) to caramelize the tops. Serve immediately.

For cherry & raspberry brûlée, put a mixture of 2 cups pitted cherries and 2½ cups raspberries into a shallow ovenproof dish. Spoon 2 cups canned or freshly prepared custard over them and sprinkle with ¼ cup superfine or granulated sugar. Cook under a preheated medium-high broiler for 4–5 minutes or until lightly browned and bubbling. Serve immediately. **Total cooking time 10 minutes.**

index

acknowledgments

Commissioning editor: Eleanor Maxfield
Senior editor: Leanne Bryan
Design manager: Jaz Bahra
Designer: Tracy Killick
Picture library manager: Jen Veall
Production controller: Sarah Kramer

Octopus Publishing Group Stephen Conroy 10–11, 23, 31, 53, 88–89, 101, 129, 136–137, 159, 193; Will Heap 1, 2–3, 4–5, 6, 7, 8, 9 left, 25, 29, 33, 35, 39, 41, 43, 57, 61, 67, 69, 79, 95, 97, 103, 113, 119, 125, 133, 139, 141, 143, 145, 147, 149, 153, 155, 157, 165, 167, 169, 171, 172–173, 175, 177, 179, 185, 187, 189, 191, 195, 197, 199, 201, 203, 209, 213, 215, 217, 219, 225, 227, 233; Lis Parsons 9 right, 15, 17, 19, 21, 27, 37, 59, 65, 73, 75, 77, 83, 85, 91, 99, 105, 107, 121, 123, 127, 131, 151, 181, 183, 207, 221, 223, 229, 231; William Reavell 13, 47, 49, 81, 109, 117, 135, 161, 163; William Shaw 45, 51, 63, 71, 87, 93, 111, 115, 205, 210–211; Ian Wallace 54–55.